THE LIVING UNIVERSE:

(The Reconciliation of Humankind and Nature, Science and Spirituality)

Matthew Irwin has lived in Britain, Ireland, Russia and China. He has worked as a nature conservationist, English language teacher, dance and yoga teacher, and historian/folklorist. He studied art and sculpture in Dublin, and dance and performing arts at De Montfort University, Leicester.

His interests include hill-walking, Indian classical dance and playing the folk harp.

THE LIVING UNIVERSE:

(The Reconciliation of Humankind and Nature, Science and Spirituality)

Matthew Irwin

THE LIVING UNIVERSE:

(The Reconciliation of Humankind and Nature, Science and Spirituality)

Olympia Publishers
London

www.olympiapublishers.com
OLYMPIA PAPERBACK EDITION

A CIP catalogue record for this title is
available from the British Library.

ISBN: 978-1-84897-144-8

First Published in 2011

Olympia Publishers
60 Cannon Street
London
EC4N 6NP

Printed in Great Britain

Dedication

The author has drawn upon many teachings and sources, which have inspired him to write this book. He wishes to thank all of his teachers and inspirers, but special thanks to Greg Cox, who introduced the author to Native American and shamanic teachings, and also his parents without whose help, love and support this book would never have come into fruition.

'May we not say that there is nothing in us during this earthly prison either purely corporeal or purely spiritual and that it is injurious to tear a living man apart?'

(Michel de Montaigne, *The Complete Essays*)

'For as long as man continues to be the ruthless destroyer of lower living beings, he will never know health or peace.

For as long as men massacre animals, they will kill each other. Indeed, he who sows the seeds of murder and pain cannot reap joy and love'.

(Pythagoras)

Preface

Science maintains that the touchstone and the measuring scale of all sound ideas and of each and every truth must lie in conformity with the scientific method (observation, testing, empirical verification, vigorous, formal proofs of physical evidence), outside of which all is inane and chimerical. Science asserts that only the scientific viewpoint can see the reality of anything. In this book I aim to show that trying to understand life and the universe through the scientific viewpoint alone is a grave error of consciousness and in effect 'pauperises' humanity.

Modern scientific ideas and philosophies are not objective, valueless and universally true as they claim to be. They are rather a preference, generalisation or philosophy of life imposed by society's value judgments. The German philosopher Engels thought that society and ideas change according to material forces, the forces of material production, which explain all social phenomena such as laws, aspirations and ideals. Ideas reflect changes in society. In the seventeenth-century European society first began to change to a machine-based, industrial one and thus the scientific, mechanistic idea of the universe developed. The universe came to be seen as a kind of machine ruled by impersonal laws of nature, which is still the current philosophy of science. But before the dominance of a machine-based, industrial society people believed existence was based on intelligences (such as God, angels or divine intelligences) rather than impersonal, mechanistic laws of nature. The Renaissance Italian thinker Tommaso Campanella (1568-1639) saw the universe as alive, as an immense living being. He said 'the world is a feeling animal.' He thought that cosmic living beings run the universe, not impersonal, mechanistic laws of nature. He believed the universe was single living organism. Today this theory of a living universe (as we enter a so-called post-industrial age) is returning in such forms as the 'Gaia hypothesis' (of James Lovelock) and is coming to be accepted by the scientific mainstream. Modern science pretends to be objective and valueless – and therefore true – but it is just a philosophy of life which reflects changes in society. It cannot claim to hold universal validity and eternal truths as its adherents so loudly proclaim.

Life and the universe are not only composed of scientific laws and dispassionate reason, but also feeling, will, spirituality, divinity, ethics, the contemplative or visionary imagination, philosophy, art, intuition, creativity and conscience. Are we to deny, ignore, suppress, trivialise or disparage values, insights and experiences of the visionary or contemplative imagination, spirituality, religion, creative intuition and nature mysticism because they do not fit into or abide by the laws, tenets and philosophy of science? To do so is to take away from humankind vital, necessary and life-enhancing experiences, values, and ways of apprehending, knowing about and understanding the universe. The scientific 'value experience' is not the only one, and neither is it necessarily the greatest or the 'truest' one. To believe that the scientific viewpoint is the truest one is an arrogant, life-denying and pauperising philosophy. It is much the same as religious fundamentalism. Scientific and religious fundamentalism both show equal intolerance towards other ways of apprehending the universe which may contradict the accepted tenets of scientific analysis or religious faith.

In this book I aim to show that the visionary or contemplative imagination, 'divine science' (our relationship to 'God' or deity), and moral science (ethics, metaphysics and our relationship to nature) are as important and as necessary as natural science for humankind's creative evolution (that is, the passing on, adaptation and perfection of ideas, insights and values, not just genetic material). To understand everything only according to the tenets of natural science is to usher in

'...an iron age,
When Fact with heartless Search explored
Shall be Imagination's Lord
And sway with absolute control
The god-like functions of the Soul.'
(William Wordsworth)

The eighteenth-century Ukrainian philosopher, poet and free thinker Grigory Skovoroda (whose ideas influenced the great Russian writers Gogol, Dostoevsky, Solovyov, Leskov and Tolstoy) thought that knowledge of the limited and transitory material world could not fill up the space created by humankind's moral and spiritual yearnings. Skovoroda wrote, 'We've measured the depth and height of the seas, the earth and the heavens, we've discovered a countless multitude of worlds; we construct "incomprehensible machines". But something is missing. You can't fill up a vacuum in the soul with the limited and the transitory.'

The pantheistic viewpoint of the Dutch-Jewish philosopher Spinoza and the German philosopher Schelling, the deism of Voltaire and Thomas Paine, and the nature mysticism of Wordsworth reveal to humankind a natural, living philosophy of life, both rational and mystical, in contrast to the dead, mechanistic, impersonal laws of nature of the materialistic scientific viewpoint.

The French Romantic writer Rene de Chateaubriand thought that humankind's desire for the absolute is infinite and only religion (and I would add spiritual and poetic yearnings) can satisfy that desire. De Chateaubriand said that religion satisfies the imagination, the emotions, inspires beautiful works of art, and contributes to civilisation. The German-Jewish philosopher Moses Mendelssohn believed that the test of religion was in its effect on one's conduct. The German philosopher and dramatist G.E. Lessing in his play *Nathan the Jew* showed that true religion allowed and provided for friendship, tolerance, communication, the relativism of God, the rejection of miracles, and bridged the gaps between the monotheistic faiths of Judaism, Christianity and Islam. Lessing believed that truth is never solid or something which could be owned by someone, but is always a process of approaching.

Artistic, philosophical, religious, theological and mystical modes of perception are as vital and necessary for humankind as scientific ones. Art and philosophy give humankind moral perspective, conscience, empathy, they help us to perceive the beautiful, and to criticise life and the state of things. Religion (the word 'religion' according to the Renaissance alchemist Henry Cornelius Agrippa derives from the word 're-ligare' or 'to unite again') unites man and God, or man and the Infinite, or man and the primary creative cosmic forces. Theology meets the needs of the soul to see the spiritual reality behind the material world. Mysticism allows humankind to see that something exists beyond mere logic. The scientific intellect searches for the nature, dimensions and extent of material things. All these various modes of perception are vital and necessary to give a sufficient understanding of everything. Science working alone is a barren search for truth and expediency on a purely material level.

Is the truth only to be discovered through the scientific method which comprises intellectual analysis and experimentation of energy and matter? Infinity and eternity cannot be compressed or reduced into such a petty mode of thought or belief. Humankind needs philosophy, art, theology, religion and mysticism to explore such issues as free will, God, immortality and the soul which science cannot or will not accept as possible, truthful or worthy, and for which a scientific explanation is not possible. Scientific analysis fills the mind with chatter, argument, words and dialectics. Scientific thought fails to 'hush the unquiet mind' to find inner stillness and cosmic unity. Science searches for a rational explanation of everything, but truth and knowledge may be gained through non-rational means such as sexual passion, creative intuition, dance and meditation. Science imprisons life in the limitations of reason and materialism. It ignores spiritual, metaphysical and moral realities. Science wants to imprison reality in a set of formulae, through abstract reasoning, in immutable laws of nature and through empiricism, but life and the universe are ever-changing, vital, creative, expansive, manifold and inexhaustible. The universe is an abyss whose depth is unreachable. Perhaps we can glimpse the truth only by letting go of our physical, intellectual and temporal boundaries. Science works with the energy centre of the intellect, but forgets, ignores or dismisses humankind's emotional centre of love and devotion, the physical centre of dance and movement, the instinctive centre, the sexual centre, and the higher thinking/emotional or spiritual centre. All these centres need to be in harmony for humankind to be whole, 'holy'.

Western science is an inversion of religion. It has its deity (the cult of reason), its prophets (Newton, Galileo, Einstein), and its devils (the supernatural, irrationalism and spirituality). But beliefs change and perhaps the tenets of modern science will seem as absurd and babyish in a thousand years as medieval religious beliefs such as necromancy and the worship of holy relics, saints and icons. Or perhaps it is not necessary to impose a single truth on the universe, whether religious or scientific, and allow humans to approach the truth, which may be manifold and diverse, in their own ways. The universe is composed of more than reason, science, accident, natural selection, empiricism, reductionism, and religious faith. Philosophy, art, creative intuition and mysticism can see beyond science and religion to give us vital, necessary and life-enhancing experiences, values and apprehensions.

Modern science did not discover everything and Darwin was the not the first person to describe evolution. The Ancient Greek philosopher Anaximander pre-dated Darwin's theory by thousands of years. He said that all living creatures arose from water, and that humans had evolved from fish. The Scottish philosopher Lord Monboddo in the eighteenth century proposed that man had evolved from wild, solitary, herbivorous, quadruped ancestors. He believed that man had evolved and had not been created by God. The German philosopher Schelling pre-dated Darwin in that he believed that inorganic nature developed into organic nature, which evolved into plants, animals and finally humans. He thought that all of nature is a giant living organism which is always developing, changing and evolving. Philosophy is as old as religion and science (perhaps older and wiser), and is able to bridge and contradict both disciplines. Bertrand Russell said that philosophy is the no-man's-land between science and theology and is thus exposed to attack from both sides. John the Scot (Johannes Scotus Eriugena, 800-877) was an Irish free thinker, scholar, neo-platonist and pantheist who was at once a philosopher, theologian and scientific thinker. He believed in both revelation and reason, but thought reason was superior to revelation. He thought philosophy was as important as religion. He believed that Genesis should be read allegorically and that God and the universe were identical (like Spinoza, who also thought that God and Nature/the Cosmos were one and the same). John the Scot believed Creation was timeless and that humans had free will.

It is a myth to suppose that intelligent people before nineteenth-century scientific discoveries believed that the world was created in 4004 B.C. and thought that the earth was the centre of the universe. This is a myth which is still put forward in scientific and historical textbooks, a ploy against philosophy and religion by arrogant scientific propagandists. Voltaire (a deist and a philosopher) in the eighteenth century writes about Indian civilisation being 80,000 years old, Babylonian civilisation being 400,000 years old, Egyptian civilisation being 135,000 years old and Chinese civilisation being 50,000 years old. Voltaire jokingly writes about the Chinese year of the creation of the world as 500,000,000,000,079,123,430,000! Voltaire ponders the thousands of millions of billions of other worlds in space, and he wrote a science fiction story (*Micromegas*) about a space traveller from a planet which revolves around the star Sirius who uses light to traverse space. Voltaire talks about the earth being merely an atom compared to the vastness of space (the Ancient Roman Pliny the Elder also wrote in his encyclopaedic *Natural*

History that the world is a mere speck of dust in the universe). Voltaire admired the Chinese and Indian civilisations for their religious tolerance and deep philosophies, but always criticised religious intolerance wherever it came from. Voltaire rejected organised forms of Christianity and the innate truth of Biblical revelation. He thought organised Christianity as it has been practised has more often led to intolerance and the opposite of what Christ taught. He said that since Jesus was born Jewish, lived Jewish, practised Judaism all his life and died Jewish, Christians would be more true to Christ's teaching by converting to Judaism. Voltaire fought all his life against superstition, religious intolerance and fanaticism, cruelty, injustice and the senselessness of war. He was a deist, a freethinker, a rationalist, and a moral philosopher. Modern science has arrogantly appropriated to itself what philosophers have always understood for millennia, and without the moral concerns, spirituality and freethinking of philosophy. Einstein was as much a philosopher as a scientist (as was Isaac Newton, which fact modern science conveniently ignores). Einstein wrote, 'The most important function of science is to awaken the cosmic religious feeling and keep it alive.' Voltaire was opposed to both religious and scientific intolerance. He wrote, 'Not that I am angry that science is being cultivated, but I don't want it to become a tyrant that excludes all else' and banishes '...sentiment, imagination and the finer arts' (Voltaire, 1735).

Philosophers have approached religion in a much more open-minded, tolerant, inclusive and searching way than modern science and religious thinking. The French-Jewish philosopher and spiritual mystic Simone Weil (1909-1943) had a 'universalist' concept of religion. She thought that we should understand each religion as expressing transcendent wisdom and that all religions are valid paths to God. The Egyptian-Jewish philosopher Philo of Alexandria two thousand years ago thought that the Jewish Bible should not be read literally (as it still is even today by some religious fundamentalists) but rather contains hidden truths found by those with patience and will. A philosophical approach to both religion and science leads to open-mindedness, tolerance, inclusivity and a more searching approach to both disciplines. Science and religion can exist in harmony through a philosophical approach so that neither shall shed their pride. But that does not necessarily mean that a philosophical approach to religion is so open-minded that it allows religious doctrines or organisations to become tyrannical, intolerant and dogmatic without criticism. Philosophers have also questioned and challenged religious tyranny and narrow-mindedness long before modern sceptical atheism and scientism. The Irish philosopher, freethinker and radical Deist John Toland (1670-1722) respected scientific inquiry yet also had a religious reverence for the universe. He wrote, 'The sun is my father, the earth my mother, the world is my brother and all men are my family.' He thought the universe is boundless and that all matter is unified. He identified God with the universe, that God is everything and is present in everything. He saw God and the material world as one and the same thing. He condemned the three organised monotheistic faiths (Islam, Judaism and Christianity) as political frauds (in his book *Treatise of the Three Imposters*). He was opposed to hierarchy in Church and State. He promoted tolerance and equal rights for Jews. He believed in liberty, equality, tolerance and republicanism. He thought politics should guarantee freedom and not merely order. He coined the word 'pantheism' to describe the philosophy of Spinoza. In 1717 he founded the Ancient Druid Order. Scientific inquiry and religious reverence are not necessarily on opposite poles as sceptical atheistic scientists and religious fundamentalists presuppose. Philosophy is about freedom of thought (freethinking) and can fly by the nets flung out by dogmatic scientism and religion. It inhabits the no-man's-land between science and religion which dare not follow it into the subliminal abyss of space, time, eternity and the inner space of the mind which have a depth greater than science and religion allow.

Chapter One

The Three Sciences

Francis Bacon, the English Elizabethan philosopher, essayist and one of the founders of modern experimental science, believed there were three 'sciences': divine science, and two scientific philosophies (natural science and moral science). Divinity or religion was the science or book of God's 'word', natural science the book of God's works (the external universe) and moral philosophy the science of humankind's mind, comprising metaphysics (the theory of existence and knowledge) and ethics (the theory of right and wrong). Bacon wrote, '...a little philosophy inclineth man's mind to atheism; but depth in philosophy bringeth men's minds about to religion' (*The Essays: Of Atheism*). Proponents of contemporary scientific materialism, such as Richard Dawkins in his book *The God Delusion*, have discarded divinity and moral science in favour of pure natural science, which I believe is a grave error of consciousness and in effect pauperises humanity.

Materialistic science employs intellectualism, materialism and 'scientism' to disclaim any form of spirituality. It takes as 'reality' an illusionary universe of ever-passing forms, which are temporary while seeming to be permanent. Materialistic science measures everything but explains nothing while all around us there are mysteries heaped upon mysteries, which materialistic science cannot sufficiently or adequately probe, dissect, rationalise or compartmentalise. What happens after death? What happens before life? What is the meaning of life? Where does the universe end? Does time have a beginning and an end? What existed before the Big Bang? What caused it, and why? Is the universe eternal? Does space finish somewhere? Why does life evolve? What created this life principle? Is evolution purposeful, directed and meaningful, or is everything a blind accident subject to chaos and chance? Science cannot properly address these issues since they lie beyond its remit of the physical world of sensory perception, mathematical formulae, empiricism, and mechanistic materialism. Philosophy, religion, poetry, art, science fiction, and metaphysics are better able to tentatively ponder these issues, questions and ideas.

Materialistic science can look at and probe the physical universe, but it falls short of anything which may exist beyond matter, since it relies on reason-deducing inferences from premises, and evidence supplied by the senses. Even the physical evidence of materialistic science can prove fallible since all material things change and are themselves thus innately fallible. Materialistic science only accepts the physical and sensory world as reality, but this world of matter is inherently finite, mortal, changeable, corruptible and unreliable. Nature and the physical universe are subject to decay, death, corruption and mortality so how can they form ultimate reality, the Great First Cause and the sole principle of the universe, as materialistic scientists maintain?

Materialistic science worships a fickle 'god', principle or abstraction, which proves unreliable. Perhaps there is a God, or perhaps there isn't, or perhaps there is a dimension which humans have understood as God beyond the physical world of sensory perception, and described by Lord Lytton in *The Magician* as '...a Power beyond the reach of his [man's] vision and the guess of his reason.' If you do not accept that this dimension exists then you end up worshipping or relying upon nature, the Creation, and the physical universe of matter for your answers about life, or upon something else, such as your own ego, money, work, a political ideology, a hero, a strong or powerful leader, or on just Nothing at all. But as the English poet Lord Rochester wrote, 'When primitive Nothing, something straight begot; Then all proceeded from the great United What?' (*Upon Nothing*, John Wilmot, Earl of Rochester) This Great First Cause, Least Understood, is beyond the materialistic scientist's visible and measurable universe, beyond human laws, interests, pragmatism, emotions, standards and conceits, including scientific laws and empirical evidence. Perhaps the universe is a mechanism that runs without any external aid. Perhaps all entity is material. Perhaps there is no soul or spirit in anything. Perhaps our universe is entirely mechanistic and material. But all that still does not presuppose a dimension or universe or reality beyond our universe and our finite, mortal, corruptible, sensory, physical and mental perceptions. Perhaps we access these other realities, dimensions or universes not through the intellect or ordinary senses, but through 'extra-sensory' perceptions, such as meditation, religious feelings, chanting, poetry, the visionary imagination, music, dancing and after death. These dimensions of being are entirely beyond the physical universe of matter, energy, force and gravitation. Perhaps this life of ours in this universe is a '...segment of existence which is enacted in a three-dimensional boxlike universe especially set up for it.' (C.J. Jung *Memories, Dreams, Reflections.*) Everything ultimately ends in mystery, and if natural science believes it alone can grasp the truth about existence and life, then it is as vain and egotistical as it is absolutist and reductionist. Jung wrote, 'Rationalism and doctrinairism are the diseases of our time; they pretend to have all the answers...Overvalued reason has this in common with political absolutism: under its dominion the individual is pauperised.' (*Memories, Dreams, Reflections*)

Chapter Two

Cosmic Pessimism

A universe which is only comprised of pure matter, has no spiritual aspect, no meaning or direction, and which is a blind, purposeless accident subject to chance and chaos is a poor and pauperised universe indeed. This materialistic, mechanistic philosophy of life leads to cosmic pessimism, as can be found in the ideas and works of such writers as H.G. Wells, Olaf Stapledon and H.P. Lovecraft.

The English writer and philosopher Olaf Stapledon believed in a Great First Cause, but this Creator of the Universe stands in the same way to its Creation as does an artist to his work. It calmly assesses its qualities but without any feeling for the suffering of its inhabitants. Stapledon (as he describes in his novels about the entire history of the universe from beginning to end entitled *Last and First Man* and *The Star Maker*) thought that like all species the human race will eventually die out, all life on the earth will end, the sun will die, and even the universe itself will cease to be, along with all life and matter. Science puts so much emphasis on the truth of matter and the hard evidence of scientific materialism but it all ceases to be anyway!

In H.G. Wells' novel *The Time Machine* the time traveller reaches the end of the world in the far distant future. He sees the last few living things on a dying earth, which has ceased rotating around the sun. The sun is stationary, red and 'baleful'. Then snowflakes begin to fall as the sun ceases to shed any light. The earth grows dark and finally all silence falls upon a dead planet. The only creatures to survive to the end to witness this final Apocalypse are lichens growing on rocks, and a kraken-like creature the size of a soccer ball living in the sea. There is a deleted portion of Wells' novel *The Time Machine* which was censored as it was considered at the time too disturbing for popular consumption. It was censored from the novel but appeared in the original serialised version in the *New Review* journal of 1895. This censored portion has since been published elsewhere as a short story called *The Grey Man*. In this censored section insects have become the supreme Lords of Creation on planet earth, not human beings, due to the enormous vitality and energy of the insect kingdom. Humans have evolved into hopping, herbivorous, rabbit-like or kangaroo-like creatures, which are preyed on by gigantic, centipede-like arthropods! This dark, pessimistic ending for humankind was thought to be too shocking to be published in the full book version.

The American science fiction and horror author H.P. Lovecraft had a darkly pessimistic view of humankind's place in the universe. Lovecraft described himself as a materialist and an atheist. He did not believe in anything other than the world of matter. He pondered upon humankind's relation to infinity and space, and came to view humankind as insignificant in the larger scheme of intergalactic existence. He thought human beings have the same significance as insects in comparison to the vast struggles between greater forces in the universe. He thought we humans are entirely unaware of these struggles. Lovecraft thought that human beings have absolutely no power to effect any change in the vast, indifferent and ultimately incomprehensible universe we inhabit. He saw no recognisable divine presence in the universe, such as God, and he thought the universe was without purpose, mechanistic, uncaring and beyond humankind's feeble understanding. Lovecraft viewed humankind as a tiny, unimportant and insignificant blot in the universe, destined to come and go, our appearance unnoticed and our passing un-mourned. Lovecraft wrote that '...the human race will disappear. Other races will appear and disappear in turn. The sky will become icy and void, pierced by the feeble light of half-dead stars, which will also disappear. Everything will disappear. And what human beings do is just as free of sense as the free motion of elementary particles. Good, evil, morality, feelings? Pure "Victorian fictions". Only egotism exists.' (H.P. Lovecraft)

Lovecraft did not believe in a 'supernatural' God but thought there might be other dimensions existing beyond our own three-dimensional universe, and other beings or entities in the various mansions of the universe beyond our understanding. Under the power of these other beings or dimensions humans are as helpless and as uncomprehending as infants. These beings or entities in space are indifferent to humankind's fate. Lovecraft did not see humankind as the master of Creation, but thought that the most rational, dominant and God-like of all beings might just as easily be glowing or invisible gases in space studying the secrets of Creation. Lovecraft wrote, 'How do we know that the form of atomic and molecular motion called 'life' is the highest of all forms? Perhaps the dominant creature – the most rational and God-like of all beings – is an invisible gas!' (Lovecraft 1916). Lovecraft attempted to explore these ideas in his stories, in which he writes about unknown and unknowable things out there in the Cosmos struggling against, or surrendering to, the Universal Whole. As Lovecraft horrifyingly observes, 'What things beyond the star-gulf lurk and leer?' These entities are as indifferent to humankind's fate as a virus or bacteria. They do not follow our earth's laws of nature. In Lovecraft's short story entitled *The Colour Out of Space* an extraterrestrial intelligence – which has the form of a coloured light or energy – arrives on earth with a meteorite. This being reduces all living things on earth which come into contact with it into a grey and brittle dust. Describing extraterrestrial entities such as this 'colour out of space' Lovecraft says they are '…a kind of force that doesn't belong in our part of space; a kind of force that acts and grows and shapes itself by other laws than those of our sort of Nature.'

Lovecraft did not believe in supernatural phenomena or in a supernatural God, but did not dismiss the possibility of other dimensions which *supplement rather than contradict* natural science's concepts of the known universe of time, space and matter. Lovecraft wrote his fictional stories with this in mind and developed a 'non-supernatural cosmic art' featuring ultra-dimensionality, not supernatural causes and effects. The 'gods' may not contradict science, but supplement it. In Lovecraft's stories we catch a glimpse of the grotesque, terrible secrets outside space and beyond time, where the 'fixed laws of nature' are suspended or defeated, where chaos reigns and the 'gods' or 'demons' of unplumbed space hold sway. There indeed may be entities in the 'shadow-haunted Outside' of space and ultra-dimensions. According to Lovecraft humankind is a negligible and temporary race compared to these entities, and '…common human laws and interests and emotions have no validity or significance in the vast cosmos-at-large.' Lovecraft envisioned our solar system as the merest dot scaled against the outside abyss of unthinkable galaxies and unplumbed dimensions. Lovecraft saw our visible world of perception and experience as highly limited and fragmentary compared to the utterly unplumbed gulfs of space beyond our visible galactic universe. Here there may be '…nameless vortices of never-dreamed-of strangeness, where form and symmetry, light and heat, even matter and energy themselves…unthinkingly metamorphosed or totally wanting.'

Lovecraft's vision of life is cosmically pessimistic and dark. Lovecraft himself wrote, 'The sciences, each straining in its own direction, have hitherto harmed us little; but some day the piecing together of dissociated knowledge will open up such terrifying vistas of reality, and of our frightful position therein, that we shall either go mad from the revelation or flee from the deadly light into the peace and safety of a new dark age.' (H.P. Lovecraft, *The Call of Cthulhu*) Lovecraft wrote in a letter in 1916 that no thoughtful man can really be happy, that there is really nothing in the universe to live for, and unless you can dismiss thought and speculation from your mind, you are liable to be engulfed by the very immensity of creation. He went on to say that it is vastly better to amuse yourself with religion or any other convenient palliative to reality which comes to hand.

Natural science which only recognises matter is a dark and pessimistic philosophy of life. If there is no God, no Great First Cause, and no karma; if goodness is not rewarded or acknowledged in the universe; if evil is not punished or has no possibility of redemption in the universe in this life or any other (since redemption, reward or punishment cannot exist in a universe of blind, chaotic, directionless, meaningless, accidental, and purposeless matter); if life is only about reproducing the species; if the gene is inherently selfish (as Richard Dawkins maintains in his book *The Selfish Gene*); and even if there was a 'Big Bang' but that Great First Cause is indifferent to the fate of its Creation, then we are left with a pauperised philosophy of life, and a society comprised of selfish individuals in which everything must therefore be permitted, good and evil, since the only important thing is getting as much out of life as possible and passing on your genes. Therefore, ipso facto, and to take materialistic science to its ultimate and real concept of life, stripped to its essentials, we are left with a world where there is only 'survival of the fittest' (to use Darwin's expression), sexual selection and competition, the power of the individual will or ego, and pragmatism. In this world everything must be allowable and possible, including economic exploitation and exploitation of nature, if they serve in the interests of the 'selfish gene'. This is a world without moral laws, where there is no such thing as society, where secularism and exploitative forms of economics are enshrined as the world's only true and realistically workable system. This is a world which has created a living hell on earth, but no other world is possible if we are only a biological machine programmed to pass on our selfish genes in a universe comprised purely of matter, and without any divinity or moral philosophy. This is the universe of materialist scientists who only believe in natural science, if they would dare to admit it to themselves or to others, since their philosophy of life cannot logically lead to anything else. Without belief in God, or some kind of divine justice, which acknowledges good and punishes evil, then we are imprisoned in a world of cynicism, selfishness, vanity, death, and nothingness. Perhaps that really is reality, but it is a very nihilistic philosophy, and why materialistic science is such a deadly, self-destructive, pessimistic, and pauperising philosophy of life.

There is an old Slav proverb which says, 'Remember you are of the earth, therefore be humble; remember you are of the stars, therefore be noble.' This proverb could be interpreted in two ways. Firstly, in a mechanistic, materialist, scientist way in that our evolution is a result of elements thrown out by dead stars, and humankind is merely a life-form evolved and adapted to a precarious, finite existence on the surface of a discrete, miniscule planet revolving on its axis and around a fiery sun. Alternatively, the proverb can be interpreted in a holistic, spiritual way in that humankind is part of the universe, the universal whole of Creation, and not a separate and discrete unit of existence. Humankind is both a species existing on a planetary dot in the universe, and connected to the entire universe in subtle ways even to the furthest star in star-filled space. Humankind is a microcosm of the macrocosm, which materialistic science has forgotten, or discarded as 'superstition', to its great pauperisation. Science has lost its connection to the real, living universal whole, by discarding divinity and moral philosophy. This loss of connection is not an advance in thought or culture or awareness, but a deadly blow to advancing humankind's consciousness, a tragic pauperisation of humankind's potential, a spiritual blindness, a narrowing of thought, and a restriction of the evolutionary expansion of possibilities. It does not – as it is claimed by materialistic science – reduce humankind to its true dimensions and place in the cosmos, but takes us to a place of restricted growth, spiritual retardation, dogmatism, cosmic pessimism and nihilism. Medieval and Renaissance civilisation was light years ahead of contemporary materialistic science in its grasp of moral philosophy and divinity, at least for the leading lights of the age – the alchemists – who are explored in the next chapter.

Chapter Three

The Living Universe

The medieval alchemists lacked much of our contemporary scientific knowledge and discoveries, and were sometimes erroneous in their scientific beliefs or theories, but they led the way to modern natural science without sacrificing moral philosophy and divinity. All the alchemists viewed humankind as connected to and part of the whole universe, and did not view the star-filled cosmos as separate from humankind's destiny, however small and humble humans are in the great scheme of things.

Albertus Magnus (the famous medieval German Dominican friar, scholar, philosopher, alchemist, astrologer and magician) believed science and religion could peacefully coexist. He was deeply interested in astrology and did not see it as superstition. He believed that stones had occult properties. Raymond Lully (the medieval Majorcan writer, alchemist and philosopher) was a rationalistic mystic. He wrote about and was interested in astrology. He believed in the unification of the three monotheistic faiths – Islam, Judaism and Christianity. He advanced the science of botany and wrote one of the first European novels. Trithemius (1462-1516), a German abbot and occultist, wrote a history of the world based on astrology. The French physician, magician, occult writer, astrologer, and alchemist Henry Cornelius Agrippa (1486-1535) believed that the natural world is linked to the celestial and the divine, through Neo-platonic participation: 'As above, so below.' He wrote a book (pre-empting feminist theory by hundreds of years!) on the theological and moral superiority of women (*Declamation on the Nobility and Pre-eminence of the Female Sex,* 1529). Agrippa worked as a theologian, physician, legal expert and soldier in Germany, France and Italy. He was denounced in his lifetime as a 'Judaizing heretic' who had the ability to summon demons. The Welshman Robert Fludd (1574-1637) combined knowledge of medicine, chemistry and physics with occult philosophy, astrology and mysticism. In those days the 'occult' sciences of astrology, alchemy, and magic, together with religious study or divinity were no less 'sciences' than chemistry, physics, and biology. Paracelsus (1493-1514), the Swiss alchemist, physician, astrologer, occultist and the 'father of toxicology', believed that sickness and health in the body relied on the harmony of man (the microcosm) and nature (the macrocosm). He worked as an itinerant physician and journeyman miner in Germany, France, Hungary, the Netherlands, Denmark, Sweden and Russia. While in Russia, he was taken prisoner by the Tartars, and brought before their leader, the Great Khan, at whose court he became a great favourite. He accompanied the Khan's son on an embassy to China and then to Constantinople. He wandered over Europe, Africa and Asia in search of hidden knowledge. Paracelsus had been described as the founding father of holistic and indeed all modern medicine, and is credited with the discovery of chemical medicines, laudanum, circulation of blood around the body, magnetism, modern psychology, hysteria and psychosomatic disorders. The most accomplished of the European alchemists was Nicolas Flamel (1330-1417) who was also a master scribe, calligrapher, book and manuscript seller. He is said to have learnt his art of alchemy from a Jewish convert to Christianity ('converso') whilst travelling in Spain. The Scottish alchemist, mathematician, scholar, philosopher, theologian, astrologer and occultist Michael Scot (1175-c.1232), who lived and studied in Scotland, England, France, Italy and Arabic Spain, wrote, 'Every astrologer is worthy of praise and honour since by such a doctrine as astrology he probably knows many secrets of God, and things which few know.'

The alchemists were not afraid or too restricted by rationality to look deeply into the abyss beyond space, time, matter and the fixed laws of nature. They knew that reason acting alone can only give us a partial and insufficient understanding of life. To understand fully and to gain wisdom, as opposed to mere logical understanding of the external workings of the universe, we need a holistic approach to understanding which includes divine intelligence, imagination and moral science as well. The Spanish artist Goya said two hundred years ago, 'Fantasy abandoned by reason produces impossible monsters; united with it, she is the mother of the arts and origin of its marvels'.

Materialistic science is too timorous to look deeply into the abyss. It contents itself with merely skimming the surface of the abyss, or fishing for facts taken from its depths and out of context, but it daren't enter the abyss. It takes the surface of the abyss as the totality of reality, and the things it fishes out of the depths as objective truths. For to enter the abyss beyond time, space, matter and the fixed laws of nature, via the subliminal consciousness, divine intelligence, and imagination, is to discover madness, death, terror, and phantasmagoria, to lose one's reason and objective bearings in a vast, subterranean chasm, where logic, mathematics and scientific laws are inverted or rendered meaningless. The subconscious universe is timeless and boundless, and contains all the latent forms and forces of all that has been, all that is, and all that will be! Yet there is also a light side to the abyss, where you can discover light (which to the rational sight appears as darkness), divinity, unity and the one-ness of everything.

Natural science is unable to '…tear the veils from every mystery – mysteries of religion or of nature, death, birth, the future, the past, cosmogony, and nothingness.' (Arthur Rimbaud, *A Season in Hell*.) Only the poet, the mystic, the shaman, the visionary and the madman – the William Blake's and the Arthur Rimbaud's of this world – can become masters of phantasmagoria, and '…examine the invisible and hear the unheard…' (Rimbaud). This is entirely beyond the remit or understanding of the natural scientist, rationalist and materialist.

The Ancient Greek philosopher Democritus thought that truth lies in a deep well from which Reason must draw it up. However, the subliminal consciousness or the abyss is deeper than Democritus' or the modern-day materialistic scientist's well of belief. No shallow pail of Reason can reach the bottom of the abyss and draw out all its truths. The abyss is bottomless. Edgar Allan Poe in his short story *A Descent into the Maelstrom* has a purported quote from the works of Joseph Glanvill about the vastness, profundity and unsearchableness of the abyss. Joseph Glanvill was a seventeenth-century English philosopher and divine who was a firm believer in freedom of thought and the enemy of dogma. He opposed the rationalism and scientism of his time, yet also pleaded for the scientific method and religious toleration. Glanvill (as quoted in Poe's story) writes, 'The ways of God in Nature, as in Providence, are not as our ways; nor are the models that we frame any way commensurate to the vastness, profundity, and unsearchableness of His works, which have a depth in them greater than the well of Democritus.'

Natural science is bound to mutable things, concrete in themselves but incomplete and transitory. Natural science is mired in external phenomena, materialism and empiricism. Scientific knowledge which only takes into account external phenomena is insufficient in itself, since the very nature of matter is mutable, limited, partial and transitory. The scientist's view of anything can therefore only be a partial view since everything is mutable. The fixed laws of nature and scientific theories are only fixed in relation to the here and now: our small, box-like segment of universal time and space. But since all matter is mutable nothing can be fixed. Therefore, as Dostoevsky once said, everything is possible.

Reason acting alone can only give us a partial and insufficient understanding of anything. Reason requires imagination, moral science and divine intelligence to give a more complete and holistic understanding of anything. Far from seeing reality as it really is, natural science and reason cannot penetrate to the core of things. Dostoevsky said that the essence of things is inaccessible to humankind, since humankind perceives nature as it is reflected in its idea or its ideal, after passing through its emotions. Therefore 'almost fantastic' themes are as equally real, and as necessary to art and humankind, as current, rational reality.

Natural science observes and then draws its natural laws and scientific theories from the material world of Creation. But this created, material world (according to the Russian writer Sologub) is a 'Fallen World of Diversity, Lust and Vulgarity'. However, 'Divine Philosophy' draws its ideas from a world of 'Unity, Calm and Beauty' (Sologub), beyond the material world. The material world is not all there is, or all that can be. Natural scientists are captives and prisoners in the Fallen World of materialism, from which they will never escape, but divine philosophers at least make an attempt to escape from the Fallen World of materialism, vainly perhaps and maybe delusory, but humans need to believe in freedom and escape, which gives them a source of hope and success, even if it proves impossible. The attempt at escape is as worthy and as successful as a real escape, since it is not the end result but the creative struggle that matters.

Natural science leads to a hopeless dead end, since if the material world is flawed and incomplete, and if natural science draws its conclusions from observing the laws of the material world, then its conclusions and theories about reality must therefore also be flawed and incomplete. Only divine philosophy and imagination can release us from bondage to the flawed, incomplete material world, and take us on wings of hope and poetry to scientifically impossible, unknowable climes beyond space, time, matter and the restrictions of natural laws. From these climes we gain glimpses of eternity, as the seventeenth-century Welsh metaphysical poet Henry Vaughan saw:

'I saw eternity the other night
Like a great ring of pure and endless light,
All calm as it was bright,
And round beneath it time in hours, days, years,
Driven by the spheres,
Like a vast shadow moved in which the world
And all her train were hurled.' (Henry Vaughan, *The World*)

Chapter Four

The Importance of the Contemplative or Visionary Imagination

Imagination is a necessary part of reality without which humankind becomes bogged down in external reality and over-intellectualisation. The English writer Walter de la Mare (1873-1956) thought that adults displayed two types or 'aspects' of imagination – the contemplative/visionary and the intellectual/analytical. Natural science only concerns itself with the latter, and misses out on a vital part of living and of reality by not recognising the contemplative or visionary imagination. De la Mare believed adults are either intuitive/inductive or logical/deductive. Natural science emphasises the latter. De la Mare said that children are contemplatives, solitaries or fakirs, who sink again and again out of the noise and the fever of existence into a waking vision. To children, facts are chameleon-like. Children are not so closely confined and bound by their groping senses as adults are. Children have a visionary view of life, which is either vitally creative/ingenious or fatally disconnected. The external world increasingly intrudes on the child's mind and frightens the imagination, which '...retires like a shocked snail into its shell.' Then the 'boylike' imagination begins to flourish, which is intellectual and analytical. By adulthood the 'childlike' imagination has retreated further, or grown bold enough to face the real world. So people become either logical and deductive (like natural scientists) or intuitive and inductive (like poets and visionaries).

The visionary's source of poetry lies within, while the intellectual's source lies without, in external knowledge of things, in action and in experience. So, adults display two types of 'imagination' – the visionary imagination on one hand, and the intellectual imagination (or reason) on the other. Both types of 'imagination' are necessary for every person to function harmoniously, and are not necessarily mutually exclusive or antagonistic, but can operate successfully together in everybody as binary opposites which can merge harmoniously, as symbolised by the Chinese Taoist 'ying-yang' concept. Natural science is a divisive and dualistic philosophy of life, and has led to a conflict between itself and spirituality/divine philosophy. But binary opposites can function harmoniously without conflict or dualism, as allowable in the Chinese Taoist philosophy.

Natural science and its exclusive focus on external phenomena, materialism and empiricism 'pauperises' humankind, as Jung said. It reduces reality to a box-like, 3-D universe, a prison of 'holy mud' from which we can never escape and in which we serve our 'life' sentences after being thrown into the world out of matter. Natural science never allows itself to see beyond its narrow prison cell of reason and materialism. However, humans have been given a key to escape from the Fallen World of matter, from the barred and bolted cell of reason, materialism and limited sensory perception. We can escape through imagination and divine intelligence. We can slay our prison guards of time, space, matter and natural laws, and escape to the phantasmagoria of madness and vision, or the garden of delight consisting of art, philosophy, spirituality, poetry and irrationalism. These are concepts and aims high above the limited views of scientific materialism.

The Kingdom of God suffers violence, and the violent take it by force. This is written in the Gospel of Matthew. I believe that what Matthew meant by this extraordinary statement is that we must 'struggle' with God or spiritual things and against the forces of materialism, the 'holy mud' of matter which narrows our vision, whether the materialism of Greco-Roman society (like in Matthew's day two thousand years ago in Roman Palestine), or the materialism of any age, such as natural science today, which refuses to recognise anything outside its narrow remit of empiricism, sensory perception and external phenomena.

Divine intelligence, moral science and the contemplative or visionary imagination are human faculties and need to be recognised, developed and used. Like all faculties, humans possess them or have developed them to varying degrees. In the same way that some people are born without or can lose their sensory perceptions, perhaps natural scientists have lost, or not attempted to develop, their imaginative faculties, divine intelligence or spiritual sensitivity. They have not learnt to fully develop, appreciate or understand these faculties. They look but they do not see, they hear but they do not listen, they think but they do not feel, they taste but they do not savour, and they rationalise things out of existence which do not fit into their logical-mathematical way of seeing things.

The spiritual faculty or divine intelligence is always present in everyone, and waits like a guardian angel to be brought out. Natural scientists have logical-mathematical intelligence in abundance, but have lost, discarded or chosen to ignore their spiritual and imaginative intelligence, that intelligence which can be used to answer why we are here and the meaning of life.

Chapter Five

The Big Bang, Ein Soph or God

Natural science takes for reality an incomplete and flawed universe, an imperfect reflection of a divine archetype. Our universe is made up of the shattered fragments of the original vessel of light, the Great First Cause, Least Understood, which broke into pieces after the Big Bang, the Creation of our Universe. Logic, mathematics, reason and natural science are not a complete concept of reality since they observe only these shattered fragments. They can therefore only comprehend a reflection of reality. Even if natural science was able to piece all the fragments together in theories and ideas, it cannot witness the First Cause, but only do so second-hand via these shattered pieces. We must go beyond observing and trying to piece together the shattered fragments of the Big Bang, and directly access the Great First Cause itself, which can be achieved at least partially by the visionary imagination, moral science and divine philosophy. The visionary imagination, the divine intelligence, spiritual sensitivity, philosophy, religion and moral science take us further into consciousness and can give us a more complete awareness of universal truths.

Whatever the Great First Cause is, whether it is an omnipresent, omnipotent, omniscient God-like force (good, evil, or vengeful), or an indifferent force which observes its Creation, assessing its qualities like an artist without interfering to prevent suffering, or is merely a mindless vortex of matter emanating from a Big Bang, unless you believe everything is chaos and has no unity whatsoever (which natural science could not promulgate, since why does it attempt to systematise and categorise everything and come up with universal laws of nature or unifying theories of time and space if everything is merely chaos?) then you must therefore believe in some kind of unity of Creation. And to believe in some kind of unity of Creation is therefore to believe in what is called God. As H.G. Wells wrote, 'Either one must believe the Universe to be one and systematic, and held together by some omnipresent quality, or one must believe it to be a casual aggregation, an incoherent accumulation with no unity whatsoever...All science and most modern religious systems presuppose the former; and to believe the former is, to any one not too anxious to quibble, to believe in God.' (H.G. Wells, *Anticipations*)

This 'God' is not a supernatural being but the one ineffable Great First Cause, the Big Bang, the creative will of the universe, the One, the All, which to us humans is incomprehensible, infinite, invisible, unknown, eternal and uncreated. It is the primordial germ of everything, unfathomable, un-revealed and of an infinite depth. I believe William Blake termed this One or All the 'Nobodaddy'. It has no form or resemblance to anything else, no similitudes, no sacred name, no letter, and no single point in Creation. It is incomprehensible to our human senses and finite intellects, the unknown of the unknown. It remains forever un-manifested, boundless, unconditioned and passive. It exists in a passive state of 'No-Thing-ness' since '...it is the nature of the divine essence neither to pass to things outside itself nor to take any external thing to itself. As Parmenides puts it, the divine essence is "in body like a sphere, perfectly rounded on all sides"; it rotates the moving orb of the universe while it remains unmoved itself' (Boethius, *Consolation of Philosophy*). It is termed in Jewish Kabbalism the Ein Soph, or eternal and infinite light, which to humans is darkness. Emanations of this First Cause are called gods, spirits, angels or demons. They are creative, sustaining or destructive deities, forces of nature, or energies. They are not immortal but live for 'one day of Brahma' or for 4,320,000,000 human years, which is the age of our universe from beginning to end (other teachings say that our universe shall exist for 311,040,000,000,000 human years!) The creator and the sustainer gods (who William Blake termed the Demiurge and the Logos respectively) together with all the lesser divinities (the gods, spirits, angels, and demons) are dissolved or annihilated with the entire universe at the end of 'one day of Brahma'. Then another universe shall emerge from the dissolution (the pralaya) to begin the cycle once more ad infinitum. Unlike the linear and finite concept of time of natural science, this ancient Indian Hindu teaching is cyclical, and the universe did not come into existence out of nothing. It is a cyclical and eternal system, and does not see the space-time continuum as spontaneous or limited.[1] An infinitude of creative

---

[1] See Illustration B

powers are created by the unchangeable, latent, inscrutable, unconceivable and unknown essence or eternal substance, called by kabbalists the Ein Soph. It expands into the visible or phenomenal universe in its active condition. In its passive state there is a contraction of the divine essence and Creation is progressively undone. The universe is dispersed and darkness 'broods over the face of the deep'. An 'outbreathing' of the unknown essence produces a universe, and an inhalation causes it to disappear. This process had been going on for all eternity, with no beginning and no end. Sufis say that there are 18,000 universes created simultaneously, so we should call each cycle a cycle of 18,000 'multiverses'! And 18,000 multiverses are created, sustained and destroyed for all eternity in a never-ending cycle.

If there is one Great First Cause then that probably explains why the concept of monotheism is such a strong aspect of all religions, even so-called polytheistic faiths. All faiths have a supreme deity, whether it is termed God, Yahweh, Allah, Brahma, Zeus, the Great Spirit, Ormazd or the Great Mother. Science itself does not dispute that there was at the beginning one Big Bang which has created everything. This Great First Cause is the primordial germ of everything, whatever we call it, a Big Bang, a God or the Ein Soph. It comprises:

1. All of infinity and eternity.
2. All of time, space, matter and natural laws in our universe and beyond it, a concept which to us is unknowable and incomprehensible to our finite understanding.
3. An endless cycle of creation, sustainment and destruction of an endless series of universes ad infinitum.

Perhaps each human being is an organ projected by the Great First Cause in order to 'see' the world in different ways? In which case, all ways of 'seeing' things are correct from scientific materialism to supernaturalism.

The Great First Cause would still exist even if nobody thought of it. It would still exist as an unknowable or unknown idea in a dimension beyond our finite universe, or our limited understanding. Natural scientists refuse to acknowledge, or seek to understand, anything beyond the visible or measurable universe of external nature. This is a limiting and reductionist standpoint. Scientists take themselves for deep philosophers, but are merely mediocre atheists, as the French author Alexandre Dumas thought. Perhaps there are dimensions beyond our 3-D universe. This idea was explained by the English theologian and author Edwin Abbott Abbott (1838-1926) in his novel *Flatland: A Romance of Many Dimensions.* Abbott demonstrated in this novel that humans can no more comprehend a fourth dimension or a fifth, sixth or seventh dimension (ad infinitum) than an inhabitant of Flatland (the two-dimensional universe) can comprehend our 3-D universe, which Abbott called Spaceland. Likewise, an inhabitant of Lineland (the one-dimensional universe) cannot comprehend a 2-D universe, and Pointland (which has one sole inhabitant, a monarch and universe in one) cannot comprehend a 1-D universe. It has been said that an inhabitant of a four-dimensional universe could see all four sides of a cube simultaneously, and perceive the whole of human history in a single moment! This notion is incomprehensible and absurd to humankind's three-dimensional concept of space, but perhaps seeing things four-dimensionally is what the gods see, or extraterrestrial entities. The British mathematician, science fiction writer and theosophist Charles Hinton (1853-1907) wrote a book about the fourth dimension in space. He developed a series of cubes which he claimed could enable one to visualize the geometry of the fourth dimension. It has been said (though probably apocryphally) that these cubes drove some people mad.

I do not think that human curiosity and inquiry can or should be confined, limited and reduced to (as natural science would have it) materialism, empiricism and a three-dimensional universe. Whether we believe in the spiritual and supernatural or not, there may be other dimensions which supplement, rather than contradict, our known concepts of time, space, natural law and matter.

Illustration B: Eternal and infinite creation of universes in endless cycle of time (based on ideas of Olaf Stapledon and Hindu beliefs)

✡ Viewpoint of eternity, the star maker, the source of all cosmic light, life and mind, eternal and absolute spirit, the star of stars, the Great First Cause

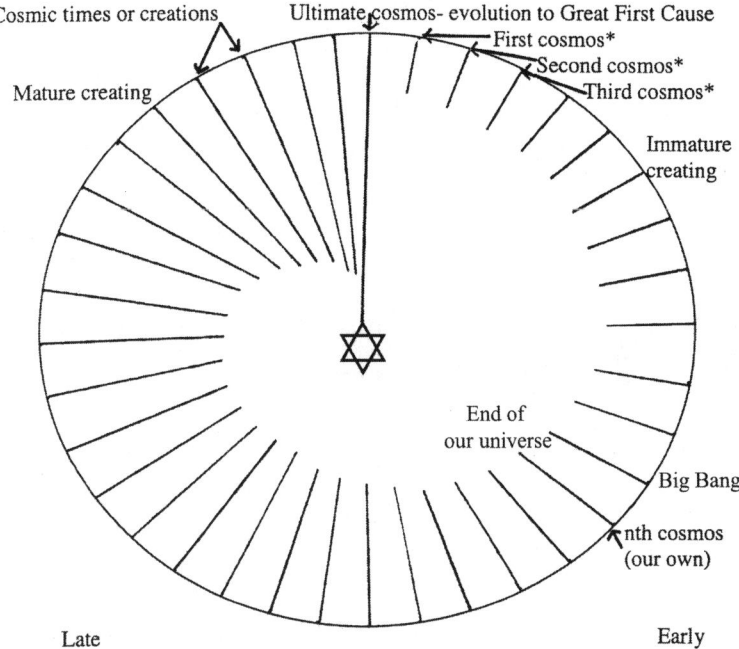

Cosmic times or creations

Ultimate cosmos- evolution to Great First Cause

First cosmos*

Second cosmos*

Third cosmos*

Mature creating

Immature creating

End of our universe

Big Bang

nth cosmos (our own)

Late

Early

Passage of time is clockwise. There is increasing subtlety and complexity of successive creations to attain complete fulfilment of star maker's capacity in the ultimate cosmos.

Period between our cosmos and next is 1,000,000,000,000,000 terrestrial years.

Our universe lasts for 100,000,000,000,000 terrestrial years

First universes are non-spatial 'musical' cosmoses of sound, silence and beats

*First cosmos- a temporal rhythm of sound and silence

*Second and third cosmoses- true life, universes of mathematical music, an eternal drumbeat

The eternal drumbeat of early cosmoses. A rhythmic cycle of 16 beats in an endless circle

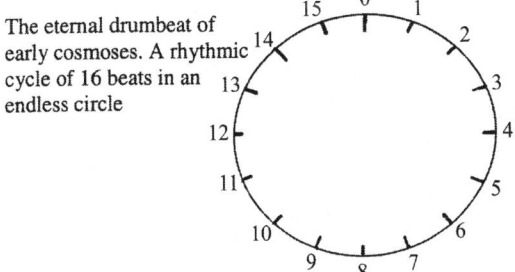

Chapter Six

The Four Intelligences or Levels of Consciousness

Natural scientists think it is 'worthless' to explore the cause of the Big Bang, being satisfied with a mechanistic, materialistic explanation of Creation, but this is not good enough. Human curiosity and expanding human consciousness demand more exploration of this matter in order to answer not only how the Big Bang occurred, but why it occurred, and what existed before. This can only be realistically explained by a 'Great First Cause, Least Understood' in an endless cycle of universes, all originating from an eternal, infinite, unknowable, incomprehensible, latent, un-manifested, unchangeable and uncreated Primordial Germ. Natural science looks at the effects of the Big Bang, but is too afraid or unwilling to examine the cause, since there might be a non-rational, non-material, in-concrete, unknowable (that is, via the intellect or empirical viewpoint) explanation. The incomprehensible, latent Great First Cause, Least Understood (the divine intelligence) willed and the Cosmos sprang into existence. The Demiurge or Creator, the active, creative principle, then directs the Chaos of spirit and matter in the universe. It animates cosmic matter by water, fire (heat), air (breath), earth, natural laws and love (moral or spiritual law, or moral science) thus setting in motion the latent potencies of cosmic matter. Thus is created the tangible, phenomenal, visible universe of matter which is a concrete model or abstraction of the divine idea. It is peopled with life, nebulae, stars, suns, planets and moons. This is the physical world of natural science which is directed by necessarianism or the law of evolution.

Adapting and extending the Greek philosopher Plotinus' scheme of life it could be proposed that the Great First Cause/the Source/the Absolute/the One/the Monad/the spirit of the universe created the 'Hypercosmic' Gods of essence, life and soul (the soul of the universe). These in turn created the Demiurge or Creator God (the mind of the universe). Then the Big Bang occurred which created the Cosmic Gods of being, nature and matter, the body of the universe. Natural science only concerns itself with the Big Bang and the Cosmic Gods, which it terms the laws of nature. By ignoring or denying anything beyond the Cosmic Gods of natural law natural science is an incomplete philosophy.

According to the Roman philosopher Boethius, everything which is known is known not according to its own power, but rather according to the capacity of the knower. Boethius thought human beings comprehend in four different ways:

1. By the senses (our bodily sense impressions). This corresponds to Bacon's natural science.
2. By the imagination (the soul, emotions). This corresponds to De la Mare's contemplative/visionary imagination.
3. By the mind (reason). This corresponds to Bacon's natural science and De la Mare's intellectual/analytical imagination.
4. By the intelligence (the conscience or divine spirit). This corresponds to Bacon's moral science and divine science, the divine intelligence.

To explain further:

1. The senses grasp the figure of the thing as it is constituted in matter through sense impressions. However, the senses can achieve nothing beyond the material.
2. Imagination grasps the figure alone without the matter – an image in the mind's eye. However, imagination cannot grasp universal forms.
3. Reason investigates by universal consideration the form itself which is in particular things. However, reason cannot know simple forms.
4. Vision of the divine intelligence is higher still, goes beyond the bounds of the universe and sees with the clear eye of the mind the pure form itself. Divine intelligence conceives the underlying forms and distinguishes them among all.

All these ways of comprehending reality use their own power in knowing, rather than the powers of the objects which are known. Therefore, all judgment is in the act of the one judging. Natural science relies on knowing something via the sense impressions and the intellect, but forgets, dismisses or ignores the imagination and the divine intelligence. Therefore, knowing anything only through natural science is an incomplete way of knowing. The imagination and the divine intelligence give us a more complete vision, together with sense impressions and reason.

For natural scientists, sense impressions and external stimuli come first in any sense of understanding. These arouse and move the powers of the mind. Scientists arrive at judgments by observing and testing (with the senses and mind) objects extrinsic to themselves. They conclude universal laws and scientific theories based on observable phenomena and empirically tested evidence, utilising deductions and inferences through intellectual, abstract, conscious perception. However, these judgments do not take into account other intelligences such as divine intelligence, moral science, creative intuition, emotional apprehension, and the imagination. Natural science is one way of arriving at judgments. In order to know or perceive anything we must know and perceive it by all our powers or intelligences, including natural science, reason, moral science, divine science, the soul, the emotions, the imagination and bodily sense impressions. Natural science alone is stuck in its own 'holy mud' of sense impressions, external stimuli, intellect and mechanistic materialism. Natural science imprisons us in space, time, matter and fixed natural laws. Only through the imagination and the divine intelligence can humankind's internal eyes be lifted to heaven and our souls lifted to sublime things. Natural science binds humankind to the 'holy mud' of materialism (as Hassids say), which is an intolerable burden to weigh us down, but the spirit and the imagination are like winged angels which can soar to the farthest reaches of time and space, and show us 'a wild, weird clime, that lieth Sublime Out of Space, and Out of Time' (Edgar Allen Poe).

The imagination, the divine intelligence, moral science, spiritual sensitivity, religion, and philosophy are God-given faculties which need to be developed and used, alongside natural science, reason, and the intellect. They can take us further into consciousness and give us a more complete awareness of universal truths. Einstein himself said, 'Imagination is more important than knowledge.' Human reason, natural science and intellect alone are unable to pierce '...the constitution of ultimate infinity, the juxtaposition of dimensions, and the frightful position of our known cosmos of space and time in the unending chain of linked cosmos-atoms which makes up the immediate super-cosmos of curves, angles, and material and semi-material electronic organisation' (H.P. Lovecraft, *The Whisperer in Darkness*). Natural science has hardly touched upon the vastness and infinite reach of the Cosmos which may contain '...strangely organised abysses wholly beyond the utmost reach of the human imagination...' (H.P. Lovecraft). Lovecraft further speculates that, 'The space-time globule which we recognise as the totality of all cosmic entity is only an atom in the genuine infinity...'

Natural science takes as reality the finite, material world, but perhaps everything that is finite and material is a delusion, and only the All which is eternal and infinite is the true reality, the reality beyond reality. The forms which scientists observe, categorise, theorise from, rationalise from, probe, dissect, and compartmentalise via their sensory perceptions and their intellect do not exist forever, nor do scientists and nor do their ideas which change over time or are lost, the world and universe themselves will cease, so only the highest and the original 'invisibles' are real and permanent 'things', beings, forms and ideas. On this little, folly-fettered earth of ours we see only their reflections distorted by our fluctuating physical and mental senses.

Scientists seek the meaning of life through the external universe, the Creation. But what may lie beyond our Universe? Perhaps there are other dimensions, more universes and strangely organised abysses. Science only acknowledges space, matter and time, but what lies out of space, matter and time, out of our universe altogether? Science is in fact religious. Science needs faith or trust (like religion) to believe in the uniformity and orderliness of nature. Expected patterns of behaviour produce scientific laws. But how do you know the results of experiment will not change in the future, or produce different results elsewhere in the universe (or outside our universe in other dimensions or universes)? That is, if the universe is even open to being understood by the finite, mortal, changeable, fluctuating physical and mental senses of human beings. Natural science cannot provide all the answers. In fact, natural science working alone is limited to human curiosity and inquiry with its fixed natural laws, dogma, taboos (against moral science or divine science), and reductionism. Natural science in this respect is rather like organised religion, but a Godless religion of Reason, Materialism and Spiritual Philistinism. Natural science is a secular, atheistic 'Cult of Reason' (which actually replaced religion during the French Revolutionary period of the 1790s).

Chapter Seven

Forever and Forever-and-Ever

Natural science examines the finite universe but not the infinite universe, the Great First Cause. The Hebrew words 'olam' and 'l'olam' explain the difference. Olam means 'world', 'universe', 'forever' or 'eternity', whereas l'olam means 'forever-and-ever'. There is a great deal of difference between forever and forever-and-ever. Our universe is forever and changeable over time, or perhaps there are a never-ending cycle of universes which continue forever. The universe, or cycle of universes, actively change and each is created after a Big Bang (Demiurge). L'olam refers to the Great First Cause, which is latent, unchangeable, passive and beyond finite understanding so is therefore 'forever-and-ever', not just 'forever' (like the changeable cycle of universes). The root meaning of the word olam is 'hidden' or 'occult' which refers to the Great First Cause, which is indeed Least Understood, and in fact not understandable to our finite intellects. It is hidden or beyond finite understanding, as is the concept of 'forever-and-ever'. Natural science can only 'see [reality] through a glass, darkly' and can only 'know [reality] in part' (I Corinthians 13:12). Natural science seeks to understand 'forever' (the finite universe, seemingly permanent) but fails to see, or wilfully ignores, 'forever-and-ever' (the unchangeable Great First Cause).

Perhaps humankind cannot fully understand all mysteries, as science thinks it can, or gain all knowledge of reality, since humankind stands as if on a darkening plain with only brief, fleeting glimpses of forever and forever-and-ever, whether by dispassionate reason, natural science, vision, intellect, moral science or divine intelligence. Humankind's finite understanding and changeable, mortal senses can give us only a limited, narrow sense of perception and reality. As the Welsh author Arthur Machen said, science explains nothing, in fact it is virtually blind, and all around us lies a great, unseen mystery – all ends in mystery. Humankind's understanding is limited enough as it is, yet scientific, empirical 'proofs' and rational scepticism wish to circumscribe that limited understanding even more, and limit freethinking inquiry about the mystery and wonder of the universe to observable, measurable, external phenomena. Human curiosity and inquiry cannot and will not be limited to such a narrow perspective. They will forever seek to break out of the intellectual, materialist, reductionist prison of science and dispassionate reason, and fly on wings of poesy and vision to unknown and unknowable dimensions of space and time, and beyond. Call it what you will – imagination, divine intelligence, or vision – it exists, and it is as real as the logical, deductive, intellectual, analytical 'imagination' of dispassionate reason and natural science. An eternity precedes our little lives and an eternity follows on this folly-fettered little earth of ours, which is but a dot in the universe, a speck of dust in a vast ocean of infinity, and this infinite universe itself is a mere cycle in an endless cycle of universes. And what lies beyond our universe in other dimensions, more universes and strangely organised abysses? All ends in mystery. Science explains nothing, and cannot (even if it tried) limit and impose its beliefs on human curiosity, inquiry, free thought, adventure, consciousness, expansion and expectancy.

Chapter Eight

Secularisation of Dance and Sex

Both dance and sex have been limited by secular, scientific belief. In Henry Miller's book, *The World of Sex,* there is an examination of sexual history, philosophy and psychology. Miller believed that the use and meaning of sex has degenerated in the modern secular world. In the modern secular world sex exists mainly on a bestial level. However, in the past sex was viewed differently. Pagans exalted sex on an aesthetic plane, primitive peoples on a magical plane, and religions on a spiritual plane. Miller thought all sex to be legitimate, and noted that the gods of old fornicated with humans, animals and trees, even the elements themselves. Miller says that the idea of sex being in any way immoral or perverted turns people into emotional cripples and leads to isolation. He believed that sex can deepen and strengthen love, or work destructively. He saw love as a creative struggle and a circle, and in that circle yin and yang (the union of opposites). Love brings opposites together for completion and unification. Miller thought that progress and scientific inventions are creating bigger and healthier youngsters, but humanity is becoming more automaton-like, a type of deified robot, which has its hands on more lethal weapons and forms of persecution.

The possibilities of dance have been limited by secular belief. It is a tragedy to think what dance once meant and how it has been hijacked by the shallowness of the Western world's materialistic viewpoint. Dance today had been reduced to mere virtuosity in ballet ('dancing skeletons performing sterile gymnastics', as the revolutionary dancer Isadora Duncan thought), and the spiritually devoid, sexualised, egotistical spectacles of salsa, jazz, popular, theatrical and social dance. Dance could and should be so much more than this, and help lead the way in humankind's spiritual and creative evolution.

Dance helps link the rational mind, the body, the spirit, the conscience, and the psyche or soul whence our intuitions come. Dance balances and heals the mind-body-spirit in a holistic way. It links us to the earth, the universe, nature, and the well-springs of life itself.

There is still in the East and in so-called 'primitive' cultures a deeper understanding of the role of dance in society. Dance is seen as much more than entertainment, virtuosity on a stage, a form of fitness, or an exclusive, aesthetic 'high art', which are only parts of its functions. Dance exists on a much higher creative or spiritual level, and serves as a form of community or tribal identity, a means of 'soul-growth', and for raising, balancing, harmonising, healing and acknowledging the mind, body and spirit. Dance strengthens the body, awakens the spirit within, calms the mind, makes you feel alive and a part of the universe.

Dance links us to our inner self, our outer body, our mental outlook, our intuitive feelings, our conscience and our emotions. Dance comprises spirituality, religion, ritual, healing, therapy and worship of God, the gods or nature. Non-Western societies acknowledge the multifarious purposes and meanings of dance, including both non-spiritual and spiritual meanings. Classical Indian dance was originally danced in the temples as a ritualised form of worship to a deity. Chinese dance, such as tai-chi, seeks to unite the mind-body-spirit and achieve oneness with the inner being and the Cosmos. Traditional Native American dance seeks oneness with Mother Earth and the Great Spirit. The high jumps of Russian and Eastern European dance are now reduced to a show of virtuosity, but in pagan times were a magical movement to encourage crop growth.

The true meaning of dance in the modern secular West has been half-forgotten, and reduced to virtuosity, entertainment, display, spectacle, high art, athleticism, lyricism, commercialism and fitness. But dance can exist on a much higher level and a deeper foundation than this. Dance connects us to our Higher Self, our essential inner being, and to the Source of all life and being, whether we call it God, the Great Spirit, the gods, Nature, the Universal Whole, the Great First Cause or the Big Bang!

In Ancient Greece dance was regarded as one of the highest forms of art and of life, for everyone. Plato wrote, 'Dance, of all the arts, is the one that most influences the soul. Dancing is divine in its nature and is the gift of the gods.' The great Russian artist and philosopher Nicholas Roerich saw dance as of vital importance for humankind, and believed it was originally the primal art form. Roerich thought that our 'primitive' ancestors had a deep and refined understanding of dance for whom '...rhythm, the sacred symbol, and subtlety of movement were great and sacred concepts.' In some South American Indian tribes dance is seen as a way of preserving the Cosmos, and of such importance that to stop dancing would mean the world descending into chaos and destruction. Hassidic Jews perform dance and movement to release joyous feelings and to worship God. They believe dance brings joy thus revealing the hidden light behind Creation. The world is mended by dance. Hindus believe the god Shiva-Nataraja (the Lord of the Dance) danced the entire universe into existence. The Australian Aborigines believe the Ancestors sang and danced all the landscapes and animals to life. Sufis (such as the Whirling Dervishes of Turkey) employ dance to reach a state of spiritual bliss.

Chapter Nine

The Godhead

Natural science confuses (and thereby debases) God with religion, sacred scriptures, divine revelation, miracles, prophecy and supernatural laws. God is beyond all these things as well as beyond intellectualism and materialist science. There are many ways to consider the Godhead including deism, theism, fideism, pantheism, agnosticism and atheism.

Deists explore the existence and nature of the Godhead through reason and personal experience, not from revelation in sacred scriptures or the testimony of other people. They believe that divine revelation and holy books are not necessarily authoritative sources, but may be interpretations made by other human beings, false or otherwise. Deists believe that God does not interfere with human life or the laws of the universe. They do not recognise prophecy, miracles and supernatural events.

Theists believe God is immanent in the world but also transcends it. They believe God is omniscient, omnipotent and omnipresent and interacts with the universe.

Fideists believe that faith or revelation leads to an understanding of the existence and nature of the Godhead. God cannot be understood by the intellect or by reason. They think faith is more important, valid or virtuous than reason in theology. They believe that faith exists prior to or beyond reason, and can include logical contradictions.

Pantheists believe that God and the universe are equivalent, or that God is part of the universe.

Agnostics think that there is no way to know about God, gods or deities, which are beyond human understanding and knowledge. Indeed, they think it is not possible to know if God exists and this cannot be answered by science.

Atheists believe that God does not exist, and the universe is a mechanism that runs without any external aid. They think all entity is material and there is no supernatural soul or spirit in anything. However, the Godhead (Great First Cause) is to be discovered even in atheism since God exists in a passive, latent state of 'no-thing-ness' which to us remains un-revealed, impersonal, immaterial, and transcendent.

I do not think anything can prove or disprove the Godhead, but whatever happiness or knowledge anyone can seek, it cannot be found in fleeting, partial objects of desire in our mortal lives, but only in the eternal, infinite and unchangeable Great First Cause, Least Understood. If time and space is circular, not linear, we shall eventually return to the Great First Cause anyhow, whether we believe in it or not.

Evidence of God or a Supreme Being can be found through human reason, as well as by prophecy, miracles, supernatural events, holy books and divine revelation in organised religions. Revealed 'truths' may be real. 'Wonders' and prophecies may proceed from God. However, one must be very careful in discerning what is real and what is delusory. The English deist Lord Herbert of Cherbury (died 1648) believed that there were five 'common notions' or universally accepted truths which reveal the existence of a Supreme Being. He called universally accepted truth 'Universal Consent'. He said there are truths obtained through experience (innate truths) and truths obtained through reasoning about experience (revealed truths). Innate truths are universally accepted and imprinted on the human mind. He believed there are five innate truths:

1. There is one Supreme God or supreme manifestation of deity in all religions (whether the religion worships gods, sacred beings, angels, saints, etc.). This Supreme God has many names and faces (whether it is called Allah, Yahweh, Zeus, the Great Mother, the Great Spirit, etc.)
2. The One God ought to be worshipped.
3. One should live a holy life. Virtue and piety are rewarded, esteemed and respected everywhere and in every age, irrespective of differing rites, ceremonies or traditions.
4. We ought to be sorry for our 'sins' and repent of them. Everyone has a conscience.
5. Divine goodness dispenses rewards and punishments, both in this life and after it, whether the rewards are in heaven, in the stars, in the Elysian Fields, or wherever else, and

whether the punishment is in Hell, in metempsychosis, or in temporary or everlasting death.

Lord Herbert believed that revealed truths exist but must be approached with caution. He said you must proceed with great care in discerning what actually is or has been revealed. The nature, quality, extent and mode of revealed truth vary and the truth of revelation depends upon the authority of the person or persons who reveal it. He said people who are depressed, superstitious or ignorant of causes are always liable to deception.

The universe is part of God but not all of God. God is greater than the matter, form and force of natural science. God is both within and beyond matter, form and force. God is both within and without the universe. God (the demiurge) pervades or encompasses all of matter and is thus immanent, but the Great First Cause is beyond matter, form and force. 'Reading' nature (natural science) is the same as 'reading' divine and moral science. 'Reading' nature through natural science has led to the discovery of the Big Bang, the Act of Creation. 'Reading' divine science and moral science via the Jewish Kabbalah has led to the discovery of the Great First Cause and the 'shattering of the vessels' of light – the 'Big Bang' of kabbalistic cosmology. Natural science and divine/moral science both agree with one another in the end.

There is simultaneously a philosophical/religious explanation of life and a natural/scientific one. The two explanations are neither mutually exclusive nor contradictory. For a full, holistic explanation of time, space, eternity, infinity, life and death, both explanations are necessary and complementary. They do not have to be antagonistic or dualistic. Madame Blavatsky said that the Temple of God is within everyone, and the one true church (or synagogue or mosque or shrine or temple) may be walled in by matter but it is penetrable by the pure of heart. You must find God (whatever God is) in yourself.

The French author, philosopher and deist Voltaire (1694-1778) said that there is a Supreme Being or Creative Intelligence or ineffable power which is good and powerful, and which rewards virtuous actions with kindness and punishes crimes without cruelty. This power or energy created all beings. Voltaire said that it is enough to know that God acts and is just. He said God reaches all places and all peoples. Voltaire said that no human being should be so reckless, vain or arrogant enough to flatter themselves that they know how God acts, punishes, protects or pardons. Voltaire did not belong to any of the sects which he said in any case contradict each other. Voltaire believed that the simple worship of a God has preceded all the systems of the world, and is the most widespread and ancient religion. He counted all wise men as his brethren and thought religion simply consists of worship, justice, the doing of good, succouring the needy and defending the oppressed. Religion is not to be found in the opinions of an unintelligible metaphysic, or in vain display. Voltaire said that a Supreme Power reigns equally in all space. He wrote, 'Should not a thinking being who dwells in a star in the Milky Way offer God the same homage as the thinking being on this little globe where we are?' Voltaire said that everywhere the heart has the same duties (worship, love, compassion, justice, mercy, etc.) on the steps of the throne of God, if God has a throne, and in the depths of the abyss, if God is an abyss. Voltaire believed that the immensity, the course, and the harmony of nature, of the planets, of the stars, all proclaim the ineffable power, creativity and supremacy of God.

Voltaire thought that Indian civilisation is the ancestor civilisation to Western culture (Judeo-Christianity). He thought that the Brahmins or Hindus were the first philosophers, theologians and legislators of the world. He believed that the Christian Gospels were fabricated and Jesus Christ did not exist. I partly agree with Voltaire. We simply do not know if Jesus really existed. However, if he did exist and if the Gospels are examined along with knowledge of Jewish history then it is evident that Jesus was a trained Jewish rabbi who practised Judaism. If you look at Jesus' teachings and sayings you will see that they are all based on Judaic and Talmudic philosophies and restatements of earlier Biblical verses (such as Leviticus 19:18; Psalms 37:24; Lamentations 3:30; and Jeremiah 29:13). Propaganda by Paul tried to abrogate Jesus' Judaism. Jesus was probably not regarded as a 'God' by his disciples. Jesus only addressed himself as 'Master'. He called himself the 'Son of God', but by that he probably meant that he was, along with everyone, the child of God, who is 'Heavenly Father of All.' Jesus was an inspired, holy Jewish prophet, a 'just man', who opposed the dogma of the Judaism of his time, the Jewish Laws and the Pharisees. He was a philosopher and a moral reformer, who spoke out against bigotry and theological dogma. He promulgated a code of ethics and taught belief in One God and one family of humankind. But this is no more than what Pythagoras and

Apollonius believed in: divine wisdom, knowledge of God and universal healing.

Jesus' teachings, doctrines, religious views and grandest aspirations can be traced back to Essene, Egyptian, Neo-Platonist and Buddhist ideas, and all these ultimately stem from Indian pre-Vedic philosophy. Perhaps the Jews themselves partly came from India, from exiled Chandalas or 'bricklayers' (migratory sects of Ancient Indian outcasts). Judaism is an amalgamation of many religions and philosophies. Jewish ancestry has been traced to the Phoenicians of Herodotus, the Hyksos of Josephus, and the descendants of 'Pali' shepherds (from 'Pali-stan' or Palestine).

Abraham and Moses were both initiates in the 'Great Mystery' wisdom traditions of the Middle East. Moses was an ex-Egyptian priest who practised the Orphic Mysteries and Ancient Egyptian rites, such as the concept of monotheism which originated from the reign of the Egyptian Pharoah Akhnaton. Judaism also received much of its ideas from Chaldean and Persian Magi during the Babylonian captivity. All of these ideas were converted to the 'masses' as Judaism. Judaism, like Christianity, has evolved, changed and developed over time, but ultimately both have evolved or been influenced by pre-Vedic India, like the Chaldean Magis, the Egyptian hierophants, the Ancient Greek and Roman philosophies and religions (such as the Neoplatonists, the Bacchic mystery school and the Eleusinian mystery school), the Buddhists, the Kabbalists, the Masons, the Gnostics and the Essenes (who were converts of Buddhist missionaries in Egypt, Greece and Judea, whom Jesus knew). Voltaire was correct when he said that India is the ancestor civilisation to Western culture. 'Greater' India (comprising 'Lower India' meaning India, Pakistan, and Bangladesh; 'Western India' meaning Persia or Iran; and 'Upper' India meaning Tibet, Mongolia and 'Great Tartary') is indeed the true philosophical, religious and spiritual 'cradle' of Western civilisation.

Natural science strives after unity and ultimately seeks one overarching explanation of life, the universe and everything which can be traced back to the Big Bang, whether it is a theory or a formula. But this one overarching Unity it seeks can be found elsewhere, such as in philosophy, in dance, in meditation, in joy, in the arts, in creativity, in justice, in the doing of good, and in religious faith or worship. All of these ways of understanding are able to bring a sense of unity in Creation which is no more or less than what natural science is ultimately seeking. Albert Einstein remarked to the New York Jewish rabbi Herbert Goldstein that he believed in 'Spinoza's God, who reveals himself in the lawful harmony of all that exists, not in a God who concerns himself with the fate and actions of men.' The German philosopher Schelling expounded a 'philosophy of identity' which sought absolute Unity as the ultimate ground of existence. This absolute Unity transcends and identifies spirit and matter, subject and object, and all separated things.

Chapter Ten

Creative Struggle

There are philosophical, religious, mystical, mythical and spiritual explanations of life, along with natural scientific ones. The Russian (Ukrainian)-Jewish philosopher Lev Shestov (Leon Chestov) certainly believed so. He believed that humankind can gain ultimate knowledge through ungrounded subjective thought rather than through objective reason and verifiability. He said that reason can be rejected in the realm and discipline of philosophy which must be concerned with freedom, God and immortality. He thought that the scientific method has made philosophy and science irreconcilable, since science concerns itself with empirical observation. The issues of freedom, God and immortality cannot be solved by science since life is paradoxical, contradictory and enigmatic, and not comprehensible through logic or rational enquiry. No theory can solve the mysteries of life and life cannot be subordinated to ideas, abstractions or generalisations. These kill life by ignoring the uniqueness and livingness of reality. This subordination of life to ideas, abstractions or generalisations leads to the experience of despair, cosmic pessimism, the loss of certainties, the loss of freedom and the loss of life's meaning. The root of the experience of despair is a certain way of thinking, which Shestov calls Necessity, Reason, Idealism or Fate.

Reason says that some things are impossible and can never be attained, and other things are eternal and unchangeable (for natural science this means evolutionary determinism and the laws of nature). Reason is seen as a sort of omniscient, omnipotent God that is good for its own sake. But Shestov thought that people cannot be reduced to ideas, social structures, mystical oneness, 'omnitudes', 'collectivity' or 'all unity'. God is unlimited by time or space, and there is a God-given freedom without boundaries, without walls and without borders. Indeed, as Dostoevsky said, 'everything is possible', even when a successful outcome is not guaranteed. Shestov believed that the experience of one's own existence is more important than rationality. I believe that natural science is inferior to intuition, and that art is the gateway to the experience of one's own existence. We must have faith in the spiritual world (since faith is all we can know about life), cunning in the mental world (since this is where society, nature, life and experience can trick us) and dogged perseverance in the physical world (since physical life is a never-ending struggle against Fate and Necessity). With this outlook, all things are possible even if a successful outcome is not guaranteed. The struggle itself is the successful outcome and to struggle with God is to succeed, whatever the result.

Shestov said that we should continue to struggle against Fate, Chance or Necessity (limiting circumstances) even when a successful outcome is not guaranteed. If the oracles remain silent, then we can give ourselves over to God who alone can comfort the sick and suffering soul. God is unlimited by time or space, and Faith releases us from doubt and insecurity through the experience of unlimited possibilities. Everything is possible, as Dostoevsky maintained. The opposite of necessity is not necessarily chance or accident, but possibility, in other words, that there is a God-given freedom without boundaries, walls or borders. Life is an 'ascetic struggle' against necessity, chance, accident, and fate. One must 'struggle with God' and not mystically surrender to the Absolute. Lev Shestov wrote, 'Philosophy is not surrender but struggle. And the struggle has no end and will have no end. The Kingdom of God, as it is written, is attained through violence.'

Most of our life is a struggle, a never-ending struggle against tedium, boredom, fatigue, petty hatreds, social tensions, enmities, indolence, callousness, useless labour, unrequited love, hysteria, neuroses, sickness, disease, ageing, quiet desperation, ignorance, petty thoughts, petty feelings, sick-minded slanders, and so on. Only our ability to endure and struggle together with a healthy dose of unprovable but comforting hope, faith and belief can see us through from day to day. Life always involves struggle of some kind, and will always involve struggle. Life itself on earth is a process of never-ending struggle. The question is – should one surrender to struggle or struggle against surrender? Perhaps both are possible to reach true balance and harmony. Too much surrender is life-denying, and too much struggle is overwhelming. Too much surrender brings decay, since the ending of passion and strife is the beginning of decay. We need passion and strife to keep us alert, active, vigorous and enterprising. Yet too much strife will wear us out. The struggle here on earth will be never-ending and only faith or hope or belief keeps us alive. It is a necessary condition of life without which we sink into cosmic pessimism, and it does not matter if it is un-provable. It is the struggle which ultimately matters whether we struggle towards the eventual perfectibility of human kind here on earth through the perfection of human society (Marxism); in a Utopian afterlife called Heaven through the perfection of the human soul (Christianity); in the Messianic Age of Judaism when nature perfects itself; in the utility of work and technology (capitalism); through art and creativity; through love and attachment; through science and the intellect; or through peace and rest after a lifetime of labour. Yet love fades; attachments end in this life or through death; the afterlife and earthly utopias whether via science, technology, or human engineering are un-provable; work becomes drudgery and useless labour; art and beauty decline and eventually fall to dust; peace and rest turn to indolence, tedium and decay; nature is capricious and mortal; and science and the intellect fail to touch or transcend the Will. So, all we have left is struggle, never-ending struggle against fate, chance, necessity, and accident. But struggle and faith unite to give us hope and belief, however absurd, un-provable or seemingly impossible, and all the barriers, boundaries and obstacles fall away, if only in our imagination, God's greatest blessing to humankind. As the English author Henry Rider Haggard maintained, 'My Empire is of the Imagination.'

The Russian philosopher Nikolai Berdyaev (1874-1948) was also concerned with freedom, like Shestov. He was preoccupied with the concept of creativity, and in particular freedom from anything that inhibits creativity. Berdyaev believed we are living through an age of darkness before the dawn of the 'Eighth Day of Creation' or the 'Third Epoch'. This will (or has begun to) involve full creative development and a new orientation in human consciousness. We have been living through a period of de-spiritualization, the devastation of nature, the disappearance of the Cosmos (through the discoveries of physics), the de-spiritualization and devastation of history (through philosophies of historical materialism), the de-spiritualization and devastation of the mind (through psycho-analysis), and the depression and shallowness of materialistic culture. Also, revolution and world wars have disclosed humankind's terrible cruelties. But as we enter the Third Epoch the task will be to collaborate with God to re-create the world in its original state, which will also bring about the healing of persons and the world, that is, the unification of subject and object, individual and society, heart and mind. I believe evolution is aimed ultimately at health, love, beauty, and spiritual ascent.

Perhaps this Third Epoch will be about the preponderance of the Greek philosopher Empedocles' Love, or harmony, in the universe as opposed to Chaos. The Greek philosopher Empedocles (490-420 B.C.) thought that the universe is made up of four elements or 'roots': earth, air, fire, and water, but it also consists of Love and Strife. Love accounts for the attraction of different forms of matter and Strife accounts for their separation. The elements or 'roots' are the contents of the universe, and Love and Strife are its variation and harmony. Empedocles thought that all living things were on the same spiritual plane. He believed in the transmigration of souls between humans and animals. He followed a vegetarian lifestyle. He believed our bodies return to the elements on death, as poetically explained in Matthew Arnold's poem *Empedocles on Etna* (1852):

'To the elements it came from
Everything will return.
Our bodies to earth,
Our blood to water,
Heat to fire,
Breath to air.'

I believe it may be that our 'soul' will return to Heaven (Love) if we lead a life of loving-kindness, or to Hell (Strife) if we have led a life of hatred and malevolence. If we lead a life of loving-kindness, hatred and malevolence (with none predominating) we continue the next life on the cycle of death and re-birth, and the soul reincarnates once again on earth in another form. It learns to balance the four elements, Love and Strife within and beyond our soul. We ceaselessly ascend and descend between Heaven, Hell and Mortal Existence, living all lives and experiencing all things, good, bad and indifferent, until loving-kindness predominates when we ascend to God on the Throne or in the Abyss where 'steadfast rest all things firmly stayed on the Pillars of Eternity'. Or we can choose to return to the cycle of life, death and rebirth once more, with its Love and Strife.

Chapter Eleven

The Imagination and the Mind

Imagination is not trivial, childish, inane or chimerical. Looking inside is as important as looking outside at the physical external universe. William Blake, the English poet and artist, believed that eternity opens from the centre of an atom. Space extends to infinity outwards and the mind extends to infinity inwards. Imagination can be as real as the 'real' physical world. We have unlimited freedom in our imagination, we can defy the whole world, even nature, and society's cultural norms of behaviour and belief, and we can keep it all a secret! In our imagination we can escape from the problems, anxieties and difficulties of the living, everyday world, imprisoned as we are in our bodies and emotions, and sink back into ourselves, into the deep, dark, mysterious, almost unexplored 'sea' of consciousness and mind. Yet this realm of consciousness is not a kind of escapism into mere imaginative fantasy, but an excursion into an unknown world, a world of the mind, feelings and subconscious perceptions. It is as important and as real as the conscious, everyday, physical world, and it is as necessary to give it our attention as it is necessary to give our attention to the outside world. By exploring consciousness we can find out what we can do with it, discover its laws and capabilities, and examine the evolution of the mind. There is an outer universe of the body and matter, and an inner spatial universe of mind and the spirit. The universal mind and universal time-space are coincidental and our consciousness is an eddy in the 'sea' of mind. All of eternity and infinity open up inwards, as Blake observed:

'To see a World in a Grain of Sand,
And a Heaven in a Wild Flower,
To Hold Infinity in the Palm of Your Hand,
And Eternity in an Hour.'

In order to explore our consciousness and imagination we must free ourselves of our petty, everyday worries and concerns, and our obsession with physical reality and materialism, since by 'getting and spending we lay waste our powers' (Wordsworth). We must conquer our mental laziness, indifference, depression, procrastination and useless labours. We must have mental discipline so as to discover our true purpose and potentiality in life, and we will not achieve this by merely skimming the surface of our consciousness. It is said we only use ten per cent of our potential brain power in everyday life. But to discover ourselves we must explore fully the mysteries of our own mind, and explore through contemplation the beauty and mystery of the world. Natural science has explored the universe of body and matter, but has hardly touched the spatial-temporal universe of the mind and the spirit. Our brain has unlimited capacities as the 'seat' of the mind. Our brain houses the pleasure circuits of sexual awareness, emotional awareness, higher intellectual awareness (such as the power of self-control and self-conquest), and also certain undeveloped circuits connected with the energies we call poetical, religious or mystical. In these undeveloped circuits are housed access to the secrets of space, time, God, birth, and death. But in order to access these secrets, we must first open the 'doors of perception' connected to the poetical, religious and mystical energies. This is what poets, artists, mystics, shamans, kabbalists, true scientists, saints and sages are enabled to do. They have access to the worlds of body or matter, mind and spirit. The German Christian mystic Jacob Boehme gained access to the world of spirit which he described as a '…Supernatural, supersensual Abyss, having no ground, where there is no place to dwell in…' (*The Way to Christ,* 1623). It lies within and beyond space and time. Edgar Allen Poe described it as 'A Wild, Weird Clime That Lieth – Sublime – Out of Space, Out of Time.'

Boehme believed that there is an underlying unity in the universe. The material universe of things is undergoing differentiation, desire and conflict in order to evolve into a new state of redeemed harmony, which will be more perfect than the original state of innocence. Thereby the deity can gain new self-awareness by interacting with Creation that is both part of, and distinct from, itself.

The French philosopher Teilhard de Chardin believed that humankind's true home is in the mind. He thought that the mind has different layers in which you can sink down. First, there is the waking physical consciousness and bodily awareness (of natural science).

Then we enter a layer of dreams and memories (the imagination). Thirdly, there is a layer of moral balance, the 'nursery' of all thought which establishes moral balance in the universe (moral science). Finally, there is 'nothingness' like the emptiness of interstellar space.[2] Here there is calmness, luminescence, stillness, and no tension whatsoever (the realm of the Great First Cause Least Understood, divine science and Boehme's 'Supernatural, supersensual Abyss'). This is the layer of the pure life energy which houses pure life and death, the death of the body and of consciousness. This pure life energy is an immense, primeval source of energy. It is what George Bernard Shaw called the Life Force, the raw vitality that drives living things. Wordsworth gained access to this realm of the mind where he garnered 'intimations of immortality' for his poems. Wordsworth called this pure life energy his 'soul' or 'inner powers'. He describes the fleeting realization of his inner being thus:

'That awful power rose from the mind's abyss,
Like an unfathomed vapour that enwraps,
At once, some lonely traveller I was lost;
Halted without an effort to break through;
But to my conscious soul I now can say
"I recognize thy glory," in such strength
Of usurpation, when the light of sense
Goes out, but with a flash that has revealed
The invisible world, doth greatness make abode.'

The pure life energy is a bodiless zone of pure mind and spirit, free of all tension which Boehme experienced as a 'Sabbath of the Spirit.' Humankind's life on earth is a combination of the pure life force plus the conscious mind and the physical body. All life is a liaison between the life force and matter. The poet and mystic is more or less a unified being since he or she has not lost touch with the inner powers or soul or life force. In the deep layers of the mind you can discover your true source of power, meaning and purpose. To lose contact with your 'inner being' or your instinctive depths is to find yourself trapped in the world of society and other people. The average person sees human society as the 'true' reality, with all of human society's little personal values, its pettiness, its malice, and self-

---

[2] See Illustration A

seeking. But the poet or mystic can rise above mere society and its superficial realities. He is part of society but also 'alone'. However, he or she is never truly 'alone' since we are directly connected to the universal power house of our inner being. Here there is to be found access to all power, meaning and purpose.

The Belgian poet, playwright and essayist Maeterlinck believed that humans live a double life, an inner as well as an exterior existence. Maeterlinck wrote, 'It is always a mistake not to close one's eyes, whether to forgive or to look better into oneself.' (*Pelleas and Melisande*, 1892)

Humankind exists almost entirely of unrealised potentialities. Even great poets, sages, mystics, and artists gain access for only limited periods to their 'inner powers', visions and 'intimations of immortality'. Humankind is a continent but its conscious mind is no larger than a back garden. But most people prefer the security of the back garden over making any attempt at exploring the continent of the mind. Cowardice, timidity, conformity and mental laziness keep them safe, comfortable, stagnant and complacent in their small back gardens of conscious waking thought. Only a few poets or mystics have half-realised humankind's true potentialities, and touched upon the great, undiscovered universe of the 'Supernatural, supersensual Abyss.' Freudian psycho-analysis can only penetrate to the layer of dreams, memories and imagination, but Jung explored further into the layer of moral balance and beyond. Jung began the first scientific, intellectual and self-critical exploration of 'inner space', the life force and the soul.

The mystery of time remains unsolved and Heidegger's question unexplained – why is there existence rather than non-existence? Are we alone in an empty universe (since the 'death of God' in the eighteenth century) or is there a benevolent principle of purpose in the universe? Is this benevolent principle the Ultimate Creator or is there still some deeper source, the Great First Cause? There is a mass of theories, philosophies, ideas and visions which try to explain all these questions, but they lead into contradictions, fantasies, over-rationalisations and produce yet more unsolved questions. Humankind is only at the beginning of its mental, physical and spiritual evolution. Humankind has only just finished exploring its own physical domain, the earth, and has barely penetrated the seas surrounding earth, let alone space. The physical universe remains unexplored, the mental universe a blank, and the spiritual universe the least understood of all.

Is the universe a blind vortex of energies with no purpose, meaning or benevolence? Is God (if indeed God exists) within or beyond creation and matter? All these amazing unanswered questions to explore, yet most people waste their lives in 'getting and spending', in useless labour, in fear, in guilt, in neurosis, in mental laziness, in conformity, in superficial entertainment, in competition, in self-seeking, and only ever penetrate to the shallowest layers of the mind or spirit! The history of most of humankind so far has been a tragic waste of potentialities but one day humankind must wake up and realise a cosmic consciousness. A few great minds or ascended masters have already realised this cosmic consciousness, such as Buddha, Jesus Christ, Mohammed, Lao-Tze, Confucius, Merlin, Elijah, Odin, Zoroaster, Hermes Trismegistus, and Jacob Boehme. Some artists, poets, writers, philosophers, and inspired scientists have seen intimations of it, such as Goethe, William Blake, William Wordsworth, Byron, W.B. Yeats, Tolstoy, Olaf Stapledon, Gogol, Pushkin, Marc Chagall, Edgar Allen Poe, Giordano Bruno, Fechner, Einstein, Emily Dickinson and Isaac Newton. Newton was a rational natural scientist, yet he was also an alchemist, astrologer, kabbalist and apostle of the supposed Ancient Egyptian sage Hermes Trimegistus. Mystics, saints and shamans can access cosmic consciousness and bring back moral truths, power, meaning, energy and purpose to people's lives, such as Jewish tzaddiks (for example, the Ba'al Shem Tov), India sadhus and yogis, Native American medicine men (for example, Chief Joseph, Crazy Horse, Sitting Bull, Chief Seattle, Geronimo), Confucian sages and scholars, Christian mystics and saints (such as Francis of Assisi and Saint Brigid), and Muslim sufis and sages.

Illustration A: The Four Intelligences or Levels of Consciousness

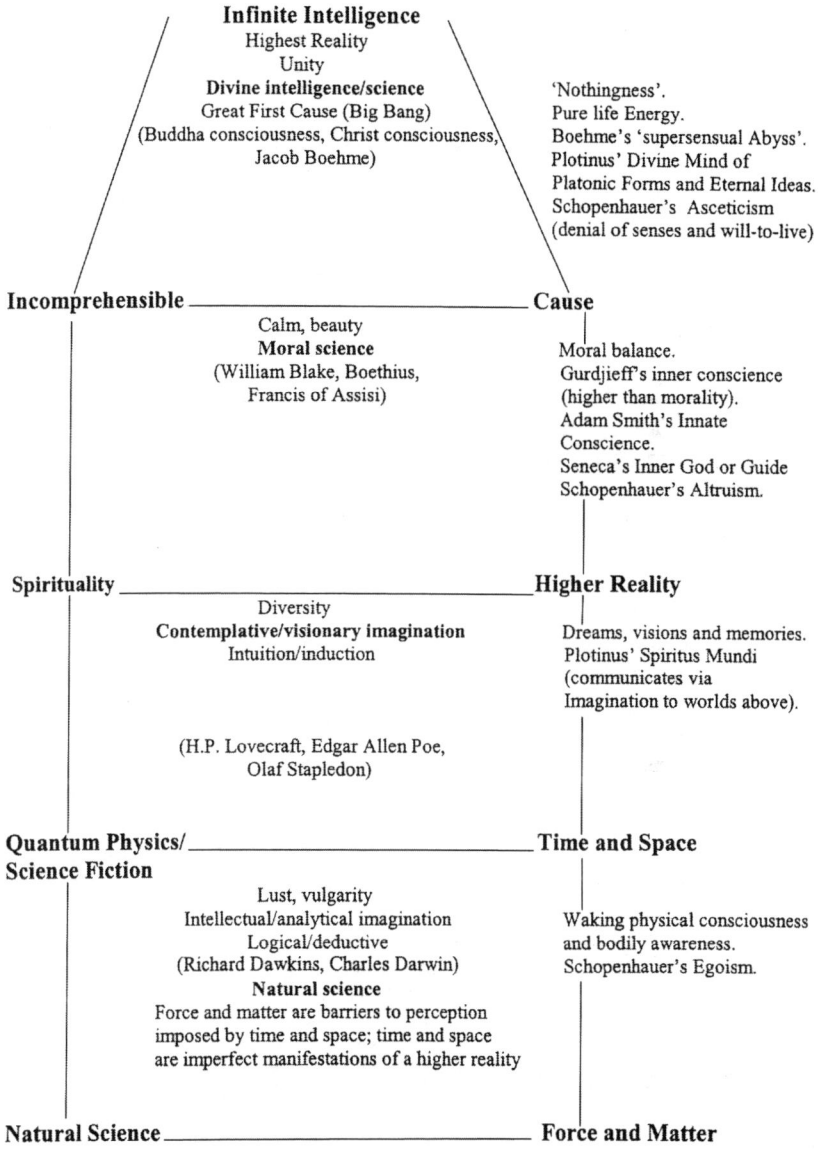

Infinite Intelligence
Highest Reality
Unity
Divine intelligence/science
Great First Cause (Big Bang)
(Buddha consciousness, Christ consciousness,
Jacob Boehme)

'Nothingness'.
Pure life Energy.
Boehme's 'supersensual Abyss'.
Plotinus' Divine Mind of
Platonic Forms and Eternal Ideas.
Schopenhauer's Asceticism
(denial of senses and will-to-live)

Incomprehensible ———————————— **Cause**

Calm, beauty
Moral science
(William Blake, Boethius,
Francis of Assisi)

Moral balance.
Gurdjieff's inner conscience
(higher than morality).
Adam Smith's Innate
Conscience.
Seneca's Inner God or Guide
Schopenhauer's Altruism.

Spirituality ———————————— **Higher Reality**

Diversity
Contemplative/visionary imagination
Intuition/induction

Dreams, visions and memories.
Plotinus' Spiritus Mundi
(communicates via
Imagination to worlds above).

(H.P. Lovecraft, Edgar Allen Poe,
Olaf Stapledon)

Quantum Physics/ ———————————— **Time and Space**
Science Fiction

Lust, vulgarity
Intellectual/analytical imagination
Logical/deductive
(Richard Dawkins, Charles Darwin)
Natural science
Force and matter are barriers to perception
imposed by time and space; time and space
are imperfect manifestations of a higher reality

Waking physical consciousness
and bodily awareness.
Schopenhauer's Egoism.

Natural Science ———————————— **Force and Matter**

Chapter Twelve

Creative Evolution

Evolution can proceed by leaps and bounds, as well as in a slow and gradual way through natural selection and competition over aeons. There may occur jumps in the complexity or make-up of organisms very quickly, due to catastrophic events such as earthquakes, volcanic activity, floods, glaciations, electro-magnetic forces from space, etc. Mass extinctions have occurred in the past very quickly, and new types of organisms have soon taken the place of the previous fauna and flora. This kind of extinction and faunal succession occurred after the extinction of the dinosaurs, during the glacial periods, after the disappearance of the trilobites, etc. I think the theory of evolution is sill barely even half-explained by orthodox science. There are so many more questions which lie unexplored and unexplained. Is evolution directive and purposeful, or aimless, meaningless and blind? Where will evolution ultimately end? Does an increase in complexity mean an increase in or heightening of quality or awareness, or just a different kind of quality or awareness? Is humankind the pinnacle of evolution today, or will not be until sometime in the far future, or is humankind just another evolutionary by-line doomed, as all life forms are, to degeneration and eventual extinction? What is the ultimate aim or purpose of evolution? Why the need to procreate anyway? Does life itself really matter that much? Is humankind evolving beyond evolution and can humankind harness the forces of evolution to direct it in the way it desires? Can humankind evolve beyond evolutionary determinism and become gods or Supermen? Will a new type of man evolve to replace the old one, which will die off in a mass extinction? This happened in the remote past, such as when Cro-Magnon man replaced Neanderthal man, and in more recent times such as the genocide of the Tierra del Fuegans, the Tasmanians, most of the population of the Native American Indians, the Armenian genocide, and almost every Jew in Poland.

Evolution and competition does not guarantee an increase in quality or awareness, since if the Nazis had won the Second World War and enslaved or exterminated all their opponents, I doubt very much that the world would be a happier, safer, kinder, more peaceful, more questioning or freer place. Evolution does not guarantee progress whether physically, mentally, morally, spiritually, socially or artistically. Evolution can run backwards into degeneration and barbarism, such as in the case of Nazi Germany. Evolution can also stand still, and no perceived change in an organism over millions of years can be observed, as in the case of the enigmatic coelacanth fish and the tuatara, a living dinosaur. Evolution does not necessarily bring about a progression into higher or more complex forms. Yet natural scientists care so much about defending the idea of evolution. For myself, I could not give a straw about evolution, whether it is true or not. In fact, evolution should actually be seen as the enemy of humankind, since it is an impersonal and indifferent force, which cares not one whit for its creations. So why should anyone care one whit for evolution? Natural scientists who defend evolution are naive, childish fools. They may as well worship a tyrant, such as Stalin or Hitler. Evolution is as indifferent, reckless and ruthless to human life, yes even to natural scientists, rather like tyrants such as Stalin. Yet natural scientists defend and uphold this tyrannical idea or theory, even worship it, with Darwin as a demi-god! They see evolution as God-like and Darwin as Jesus Christ.

Life and evolution is far more complex than Darwin's theory allows. Life has far more potential, beauty, complexity, awe, wonder, poetry, energy and meaning than simply being an agency of genetically-bounded material imprisoned by sexual competition and natural selection. And if life really is that constrained, then evolution is an enemy to be either destroyed or captured as an idea, then tamed and harnessed for humankind's betterment, and finally liquidated altogether. Are humans slaves to evolution or shall we be masters of it? Anyhow, why bother to evolve into new forms, would it not be better to become immortal gods and keep the same form forever? Or is changelessness as bad as listening to the same piece of music over and over again? If humans do ultimately gain cosmic consciousness and total evolution, what then? Shall we contemplate life and/or nothing-ness totally free of passion, strife and desire, or actively create a universe and involve ourselves in it, like God? Whither life? Whither humankind? All ends in mystery. Natural science explains nothing.

If time itself comes to an end, then what happens at the final moment – a bang, a whimper, nothingness, or an eternal and glorious 'eternal now' when no more time shall be, and when an infinite and eternal cosmic consciousness shall reign? Is the object of evolution an increase in consciousness anyway? How does that increase in consciousness work? Is humankind evolving in ever-increasing consciousness collectively, or rather can certain individuals 'speed up' evolution and reach cosmic consciousness in their own lifetime? Is this what happened to the great people of history – the artists, poets, writers, musicians, dancers, inspired natural scientists, visionaries, sages, seers, mystics, saints, sufis, kabbalists, shamans, etc? Natural science working alone is a shallow philosophy when it boils down to the mystery of life itself. Perhaps evolution is a local, specific principle of life only applicable to our own planet earth, or our own galaxy. Can evolution be applied universally, even to other dimensions? Perhaps there is life in space or in another dimension which is beyond evolution, and perhaps this is what is meant by the gods, and God is the eternal and infinite Great First Cause of evolution, the star-maker, the Great Spirit behind, above, below, within, preceding, directing, initiating, observing and allowing evolution. Evolution is a great, fluid, creative flow of life to be encompassed not only as a wasteful, strife-ridden, selfish, genetic competition as in Darwin's theory but also as a creative process of beauty, wonder, awe, purpose, unity, bountifulness, love and spirit.

The German psychophysicist and psychologist Gustav Fechner (1801-1887) saw the whole universe as alive – the plants, the animals, the earth, the planets, and the stars. Fechner thought the whole universe is a living being. He believed humankind stands midway between the souls of plants and the souls of stars, which are what we call angels. God is the soul of the universe. He thought natural scientific laws are merely modes of the unfolding of God's perfection. He compared this joyous 'daylight view' to the dead, dreary 'night view' (what I call cosmic pessimism) of materialism. He viewed God as the totalised consciousness of the whole universe, of which the earth's consciousness forms an element, just as in turn each human consciousness forms an element of the whole earth's consciousness.

Fechner's concept of the stars as live, conscious beings with souls is mirrored in the writings of the English science fiction author Olaf Stapledon, such as in his novel *Starmaker*. Maimonides, the medieval Spanish-Jewish scholar, also thought that the celestial bodies were living, animated beings. The Belgian author Maeterlinck (like Fechner) extended consciousness to plants, and intelligence to insects. In Maeterlinck's book *The Intelligence of Flowers* (1907) he proposes that plants have wisdom and self-interest. In his book *The Life of the Bee* (1900) Maeterlinck describes a bee's life as one of intelligent co-operation, work and a reasoning mind in their social life. Whether it is called 'instinct' or 'intelligence' a bee's consciousness is of a cosmic nature, an emanation of the universal soul.

The sixteenth-century philosopher, priest, cosmologist and occultist Giordano Bruno conceived that the universe is a kind of infinite living being. For ideas such as this Bruno was burnt at the stake for heresy by the Catholic Church. Modern scientific materialist inquisitors would burn Bruno at an intellectual stake today for his ideas. Bruno believed God is not a remote heavenly deity but an immanent being and present on the earth as in the heavens. God subsumes in itself the multiplicity of existence. God has no particular relation to one part of the infinite universe more than any other. The universe is made of four elements (earth, air, fire and water) plus the universal spirit or 'ether'. Bruno wrote, 'I cleave to the heavens, and soar to the infinite.' Perhaps Bruno's 'ether' or universal spirit is what George Bernard Shaw called the 'Life Force', William Wordsworth called the 'inner powers' or 'soul', Shelley called the 'Power which is seated upon the throne of my own soul', Maeterlinck called the 'universal soul', Boehme called the 'supernatural, supersensual Abyss', and Edgar Allen Poe called the 'Wild, Weird Clime that Lieth Sublime Out of Space and Out of Time.'

I believe that art and creativity are humankind's greatest achievements. Art and creativity are God-like powers, since you are co-creating with the Creator, and touching or transcending the will, as the German philosopher Schopenhauer put it. True art is above commerce, business, politics, power-for-power's-sake, hierarchical social authority, science, the intellect, even philosophy and sexual prowess. Artists are demi-gods! Artists have the true upper hand in life, whether poor or rich, humble or powerful, famous or unknown, since only artists can touch or transcend the will. All work and business is useless labour in comparison to artistic creativity, which equals spirituality, since you are co-creating with God. The Belgian writer Georges Duhamel maintained that true civilisation can only be based on the human heart and creativity, not as it is on technological progress and money-grabbing. He dedicated his life to literature and defending human civilisation. There is no truer aim in life than this.

The nineteenth-century German philosopher Schopenhauer believed that it is not through science, philosophy or logic that humankind can gain an insight into the infinite and the universal. Schopenhauer put art, loving-kindness, and spiritual or religious discipline above science, logic and philosophy. Schopenhauer believed that the thinking subject could only be jarred out of his limited, individual perspective through the medium of art, in which he could feel a sense of the universal directly. Schopenhauer believed the universal was the 'Will', and the Will was the inner content or driving force of the world. Schopenhauer thought that discursive thought (science, philosophy, and logic) could neither touch nor transcend the nature of desire, which eternally torments humankind. Art, on the other hand, is a spontaneous act which cannot be linked to either body or intellect. Art is a spontaneous, pre-determined idea which the artist has in his mind before even attempting to create it. Art places humankind above science and ultimately nature since it goes beyond the realm of sufficient reason. Schopenhauer believed that science can be relegated to the boundaries of reason, and that genius is precluded from entering its territory. Schopenhauer thought that the ability to view nature aesthetically is a telltale sign of genius.

Chapter Thirteen

Death

What happens after death? Is there a Hell for sinners and a Heaven for the redeemed? Is the idea of Heaven or Hell a religious myth? Do sinners suffer in Hell for eternity? Jewish teachings view the afterlife in a very enlightened way. They speak of an abode called 'Sheol' (like Hades in the Greek myths) which is the abode of all the dead, and 'Gehenna' (like Tartarus, the deepest Hell, in the Greek myths), which is a fiery hell for the wicked, who suffer and repent there for a period of twelve earthly months in time. They then go to Sheol. In Jewish teachings there is no eternal damnation, devil or Satan, and nobody suffers in hell for all eternity.

Messianic Jewish teachings say that all the dead (the evil in Gehenna and the good in the 'bosom of Abraham' in Sheol) shall be raised in the Messianic Age when death shall be no more. Mystical Jews and Hassidim believe in the transmigration of the soul, like Hindus (ancient Hindu teachings say that we all have 84 million lifetimes). Instead of a resting place in Gehenna mystical Jews believe the soul reincarnates on earth until the Messianic Age. Two thousand years ago the Jewish writer and priest Josephus wrote, 'All pure and holy spirits live on in heavenly places, and in course of time they are again sent down to inhabit righteous bodies.' Josephus says that reincarnation was commonly accepted among Jews of his time.

In the Jewish author Sholem Asch's novel *The Nazarene* there is a description of the workings of reincarnation. The soul passes through the 'sea of forgetfulness' from one life to another. The 'Angel of Forgetfulness' removes from our memories the records of the former life. Sometimes the Angel of Forgetfulness forgets to remove all the memories of our past lives, which come to haunt us as fleeting dreams and memories half-perceived in our thoughts.

The Ancient Greeks, like the Jews and Hindus, took the idea of reincarnation seriously. For example, Pythagoras advocated the doctrine of 'new birth' or metempsychosis whereby at death the soul passes into another living creature.

Chapter Fourteen

The Will to Power and Self-Knowledge

In order to creatively evolve and free ourselves of cosmic pessimism and despair humans must constantly struggle and work on themselves to gain self-knowledge. This was advocated by the philosophers Nietzsche, Gurdjieff and Zeno.

The nineteenth-century German philosopher Nietzsche thought that we could overcome despair and creatively evolve in three ways. Nietzsche believed that all humans possess the will to power. The will to power involves a struggle against one's surroundings to gain, for example, personal growth, self-perfection, power, expanded consciousness, love, creativity, and even the dispassionate search by natural science for objective, absolute truth whether life-affirming or nihilist. We can use the will to power in three ways. Firstly, by using the will to power destructively, in the rejection of, and rebellion against, societal ideas and moral codes which dis-empower and restrict our growth. Secondly, by using the will to power creatively, in overcoming nihilism and re-evaluating old ideals or creating new ones, and thirdly, by a continual process of self-overcoming. Nietzsche thought that one must take absolute responsibility for oneself, including what is terrible or questionable. He believed that modern, democratic society produces a tendency to equality, which homogenises all beings and ultimately leads to nihilism. Nietzsche maintained that aristocratic societies such as Ancient Greece or Renaissance Italy produced more creative individuals than modern democracies.

The Russian-Greek-Armenian philosopher Gurdjieff believed humans must continually work on their inner selves to become fully awake. He said we should try to free ourselves from the 'waking sleep' of ordinary consciousness. We can waken to higher levels of consciousness, by utilising methods to increase and focus our attention and energy, and by minimising daydreaming and absent-mindedness.

Gurdjieff thought everybody has an inner conscience which is higher than morality. He said that morality is culturally contrived, contradictory and superficial.

The Ancient Greek philosopher Zeno believed in self-development. He said, 'Man conquers the world by conquering himself'. He said that humans must have self-control against life's vicissitudes and that we must learn how to steel our sensibilities, so that life will hurt us as little as possible.

Chapter Fifteen

'Magic' and the Imagination

Mystical, religious, artistic or intuitive realisations are not inane or chimerical. The world's greatest minds have admitted and embraced what we call 'magic', mysticism, universal wonder and awe including Isaac Newton (who was an alchemist, astrologer, kabbalist and disciple of the Ancient Egyptian sage Hermes Trismegistus), Albert Einstein (who said that imagination is more important than knowledge), William Blake, H.G. Wells, Plato, Pythagoras (an initiate of the Greek Mystery Schools), Archimedes (an initiate of the Greek Mystery Schools), Carl Jung and the Romantic poets.

At the end of the nineteenth century in the British Isles some of the most brilliant minds of that era formed the Order of the Golden Dawn, a secret society of Rosicrucian inspiration, which practised ceremonial magic and the acquisition of initiatory knowledge and powers. Its members included the Irish poet, dramatist and Nobel prize winner W.B. Yeats, the authors Algernon Blackwood and Bram Stoker, Peck (the Astronomer Royal of Scotland), Allan Bennett (a celebrated engineer), Sir Gerald Kelly (the President of the Royal Academy), the extraordinary 'black magician' Aleister Crowley, Florence Farr (the Director of the Abbey Theatre and a close friend of George Bernard Shaw), and the famous writers Arthur Machen, M.P. Shiel and Sax Rohmer. This secret society sprang from earlier magical societies such as the English Rosicrucian Society (whose members included the celebrated English author Bulwer-Lytton). It had affiliations with similar German societies, which later evolved into the German philosopher, educator and writer Rudolf Steiner's anthroposophical movement.

The world's greatest and most brilliant minds have not rejected or dismissed spirituality, the imagination, or the idea and practice of 'magic'. Magic is to be distinguished from the merely 'occult' or supernatural, which attempts to mystify, and is therefore a pseudoscience. Natural science neglects or ignores the power of the human mind to alter or change circumstances and conditions, but this narrow approach limits human potentiality and possibilities. Who can say what 'Mirrors of the gigantic shadows which futurity casts upon the present' (Shelley) we might peer into, if we were to expand or enlarge our consciousness, and stop subordinating the question of meaning to the mere 'accumulation of facts and calculating processes' (Shelley) of positivist natural science. Natural science keeps humankind in an 'un-awakened' state, through fear, ignorance of the real cause of things, lack of foresight, and narrow materialist philosophies. If humankind could envisage and construct a society with a 'just distribution of the produce which [the science of economics and technological advancements] ...multiplies' (Shelley) then humankind could have the time, leisure, resources, freedom, and material abundance to develop and expand the potentially unlimited powers and possibilities of the human mind, body and spirit. It is both reason and superstition which stand in the way of humankind's unlimited potentialities and help to obscure totality of vision. A human being must break down all the rational and superstitious barriers, walls, and boundaries which prevent him or her from leading a full and abundant life mentally, physically and spiritually. It is 'our meddling intellects' and small minds which 'mis-shape the beauteous forms of things' and 'murder to dissect.' When we bring with us a 'heart that watches and receives [nature] ' (in the words of Wordsworth) we perceive and receive totality of vision, the universal energy of chi, or prana, or vril (as imaginatively termed in Bulwer-Lytton's novel *The Coming Race*) or what James Joyce referred to as an 'epiphany.'

Chapter Sixteen

Divine Inspiration and Creativity

If time and space are circular and infinite rather than linear (as generally perceived in Western science and thought) then all of humankind has the possibility of access to the infinite, to the eternal and to totality of vision. The Great First Cause (or the Source, Brahma, the Great Spirit, the Big Bang) 'sits' at the 'centre' of the universe watching or contemplating Creation unfold. The time/space continuum which is circular and rhythmic spins around the Great First Cause. It is 'danced' or 'drummed' or 'spoken' into Creation by a Demiurge (such as Shiva, Yahweh, Odin, Allah, the Whitechrist, etc) who kicks away the dust of Chaos. Totality of vision or the 'Eternal Now' in mystical or religious experience is when the space-time continuum moves closer to the source and when we receive inspiration (by moving closer to the centre or Source).

Western society today has gone too far down the road of materialistic, 'positivist' science. Positivist science wishes to confine all inquiry about life and the universe to observable facts derived from empiricism, logic, the intellect and the senses. But can we rely solely on the intellect and the senses for all understanding? Humankind's life is temporary, mutable, finite, and everything that exists is open to interpretation and multiple layers of meaning, perhaps beyond the intellect or the senses. For positivist scientists metaphysics, theology and philosophy are ignored or seen as illegitimate. Positivist science fosters intellectual distancing from the sense of wonder or awe at the beauty and complexity of the Creation, our connection to the living universe, and totality of vision. Perhaps reason and the intellect hide the real world from our eyes. No matter how much we know it can only breed a sense of wonder – 'to know can only wonder breed, and not to know is wonder's seed.'

Humankind's greatest asset is not reason or the intellect but the imagination, vision and the sense of wonder. To 'imagine' means to 'image', to form a vision or 'image' in the mind's eye and then to use this image to work 'magic'. Magic and imagination are derived from the same word: 'mage'. A mage is a magician who uses his or her imagination to work miracles. The American author Sherwood Anderson thought that in the beginning when the world was young there was no truth, only vague thoughts. Man made truth from his thoughts, his imagination. He did this through the power of magic and vision, and these 'made' truths do not have to be cast in stone eternally. The artist, the magician, the mage, and the shaman create truths or realities by co-creating with the Creator. This is creative evolution. Humans are not as powerless as Darwin believed. We are not completely bound in chains by our genes, our environment, natural selection, sexual competition, survival of the fittest, but can rise above these restrictions and become (as Nietzsche believed) supermen or magicians, and co-create with the Creator. Man is born free, as Rousseau said, but is everywhere in self-created chains. One of the links in those chains is reason, another positivist, materialist science, another Social Darwinism, and another the intellect. These limit humankind's vision and sense of possibility in life. Materialist, positivist science and organised religion are means of intellectual and social control, and try to prevent, block or denigrate the power of the imagination. You are only allowed to imagine so far and no further. Materialist science only allows the imagination to stay within empirical evidence and observable facts. Organised religion only allows the imagination to stay within certain accepted dogma or the revealed truths of certain prophets. But humankind can look beyond both materialist science and organised religion and see further. Not to see further is to block humanity's soul growth, and dam the wells of inspiration and creative evolution. Materialist science relies on the intellect and the senses, but the intellect and the senses are unreliable, as can be experienced using hallucinogenic drugs and in cases of schizophrenia. The senses and the intellect are not to be trusted, since they are in a constant state of change, both during the lifetime of an individual and through historical time. At the end of the day, reason, materialist science, and logic are just certain kinds of thought-patterns, by-products of the mind and spirit.

To be a creative artist is to go further, to co-create with the Creator, to realize one's will to power, and to challenge society's conventional wisdom and norms, which are culturally contrived and historically bound. You must break free of the chains of society, nature and culture in order to be born again via a search inward. Materialist science and organised religion put blocks on the imagination, the will to power and creative evolution. They do this through the use of fear, but life only expands according to one's courage. Science and religion cause life to shrink, by saying that if you do or believe such-and-such then such-and-such will happen or result (you will be damned, lost or deluded), so you must follow a delineated path of strict orthodoxy in religious or scientific beliefs. Science fears irrationality, and religion fears reason. But that is just being bound and repressed by a limiting idea of what is and isn't possible. You are being told beforehand how far you can or cannot go. But all leaps in consciousness require imagination. As the Russian author Herzen reminds us, '…every aspiration for the future involves some degree of imagination; and but for unpractical people, practical life would never get beyond a tiresome repetition of the old routine.'

The search for truth or reality cannot and will not be bound by the limiting ideas of materialist science and organised religion, which instil doubt and fear. As William Blake said, 'If the Sun and Moon should doubt, they'd immediately go out.' The Sun and Moon of Truth know no limits, doubt or fear. To understand as much as possible is the primary search for truth, and 'everything that is understood is good' (Oscar Wilde). There are more truths in heaven and earth than is understood in the philosophies of organised religion and materialist science. Human nature and the laws of nature are encoded in the narrative of religion, science and myth, as pointed out by Francis Bacon in his book *The Wisdom of the Ancients* and in the works of Joseph Campbell. But the human mind, body and soul have greater capabilities than the narratives of science, religion and myth allow.

Science limits human possibilities by only allowing reason and empiricism to guide human affairs or self-knowledge. Religion limits possibilities by solely relying on dubious revelation, and by dividing good from evil through subjective prohibition, or the deferred gratification of desire. Science relies on reason, logic and empiricism to decide what can or cannot exist, and religion relies on certain revelations to decide the truth. But these truths of religion or science are conditional truths, but truth or reality cannot be conditional on anything. Truth and reality are above and beyond conditionality, materialist circumstances or revealed laws. Truth and reality are to be found in the free life of the imagination.

Truth cannot be subject to the slumber of materialism and empiricism, or religious prohibitions, or coerced into institutionalised, hierarchical socio-economic systems, where poverty is created in the midst of plenty, and ethics is corrupted by economic competition and selfish individualism. It is humankind's way of thinking which is at fault. We must change our way of looking at the world. We must aim for spiritual elevation and intense delight in the divinity which permeates all Creation, as revealed in the poems of Thomas Traherne. Perhaps a naive and simple philosophy, but better than striving after comforts or acquisitions that bring no comfort to the heart. Organised religions, materialist science, determinism, reductionism, and economic competition leave no room for the free play of the imagination, joy, creative evolution, and soul growth.

Chapter Seventeen

The Divine Masculine and the Divine Feminine

I believe that most organised religions for the past two thousand years have displaced, outlawed and repressed the sacred or divine feminine. Materialist science in its turn over the past three hundred years has lost, discarded, ignored and forgotten both the divine feminine and the divine masculine. Patriarchal religions displaced or contained (within such figures as Kali, Brigid, the Mother of God, the Shekinah, etc) the sacred feminine two millennia or more ago. Materialist science rejected the idea of the universe as a living, vital presence with sacred attributes such as the divine masculine and feminine, and replaced them with a universe of lifeless, inert matter. We have therefore today in both secular and religious societies a loss of certain meanings and connections. Apollo, for example, who was the Ancient Greek god or patron figure of poetry, music, dance and the arts, along with Pan who was the horned god of nature (vilified by Christianity as the devil or Satan), as well as Pallas Athene who was the goddess of war, wisdom and the arts, and Gaia or mother earth have all been trivialised, demonised, and reduced to mere myth and fancy. Thus we are able to exploit with impunity the earth and its resources since it is just 'de-sacralised', inert, lifeless matter to feed the insatiable demands of a techno-industrial world civilisation. Witches or 'wise women' were physically annihilated in their millions by zealous patriarchal organised religions. Poetry and dance have been trivialised or feminised by techno-industrial societies in comparison to more practical disciplines. The sacredness of both the masculine and the feminine have been eroded, trivialised, corrupted, divided and repressed by organised religions and secular societies. But as Virginia Woolf once advised, '...the woman part of a man's brain must have effect in a man, and a woman must have intercourse with the man in her...' if the individual is to be whole. This is the Tao, the Divine Androgyne, the fusion of opposites, and the Alchemist's or

Philosopher's Stone. This fusion of opposites leads to wholeness, 'holi-ness', and totality of vision. The English poet Coleridge believed that a great mind must be androgynous, both active and passive. He thought that creativity is passive in the sense that flashes of insight and inspiration emanate from the soul or higher self to the 'brain-womb' through spiritual intercourse with nature, history and the Muse.

Chapter Eighteen

Modern Science and Poetry Evolved from Goddess Worship

The true scientist (astronomer/mathematician), artist, poet, writer, musician and dancer are inspired by the 'Goddess as Muse'. The High Poet of the Ancient World was the servant of the High Priestess, who was the highest-placed living person in the Goddess temples. The Ancient Greek writer Homer is an example of a High Poet of the Goddess. Poetry comes from the 'Goddess as Muse', which many poets and writers throughout history have written about, including William Shakespeare, Christopher Marlowe, Edmund Spenser, Geoffrey Chaucer, John Milton, Ben Jonson, J.W. Goethe, Friedrich Schiller, Dante Alghieri, Samuel Taylor Coleridge, William Wordsworth, John Keats, P.B. Shelley, Dante Gabriel Rossetti, Algernon Swinburne, Rainer Maria Rilke, W.B. Yeats and Robert Graves. Science, poetry, music and dance are more than a profession or a hobby, but a personal relationship with the Divine, as they were for the High Poets of the ancient Goddess temples. Poetry comes from the Goddess and serves to bring her near. Robert Graves wrote, 'The function of poetry is the religious invocation of the Muse; its use is the experience of mixed exaltation and horror that her presence excites...'

According to an old Irish poem it is death to mock a poet because he has the power of great knowledge, is favourite to the 'Queen of Heaven' and thus has supernatural powers; it is death to love a poet because he is distracted by his affair with the Goddess, and so makes a poor husband; and it is death to be a poet because he has made himself a sacrifice to the Goddess. The poets and High Druids of Ancient Ireland held the secret of writing. They kept inscriptions of the alphabet (probably ogham) in secret crane-skin bags. Poetry, maths, astronomy and writing were powerful magical tools used by the poets and the Druids with the help of the Goddess. The crane or heron was sacred to the Goddess. Pythons were also sacred animals in the ancient

Goddess temples of the Mediterranean and Middle East. The High Priestess of the temple was called a Pythoness, snake-holder or Ophicius. The High Priestess is often depicted as a bare-breasted woman holding two snakes. Poets, musicians, astronomers and mathematicians contended for the Goddess' favours, which meant glory in this life and after death in the eternal stars. The Goddess was seen as the lover, mother and nurturer of humankind, and the layer-out of humankind when the individual returns in death to the unknown.

The Etruscans of Ancient Italy were Goddess worshippers. Their Great Goddess Minvra became Minerva or Athena under the Romans, the goddess of warriors, poetry, music, wisdom, medicine, and crafts. The famous Ancient Greek female poet Sappho of Lesbos was a Goddess worshipper and a High Priestess of Lesbos. Sappho contacted the 'Goddess as Muse' through the messenger and servant of the Goddess, Hermes.

The successors to the High Poets were the Druids, the medieval Cabbalists and the Romantic poets. The Cabbalists invoked Hermes Trismegistos ('Thrice-Great Hermes'). The Druids had sacred groves, natural rock formations or stone pillars dedicated to the Goddess and open to the moon (the moon was sacred to the Goddess). They served as Goddess temples. Julius Caesar wrote that the Druids were skilled astronomers and astrologers, knew the size of the earth and of the universe, and the order of nature.

The last recorded High Priestess (who was also a skilled mathematician) was Hypatia of Alexandria who was flayed alive by a mob of Christian fanatics in the second-century A.D. She was the daughter of the Goddess temple mathematician Theon, who was the last recorded High Poet of the Goddess. Astronomy, medicine, maths, dance, art, poetry and music developed in the Goddess temples of Iraq, Crete, Etruria (the Etruscans), Greece and Grecian Egypt. This skill and knowledge was passed to Arab cultures and the Druids in Ireland, and from Arab cultures and Irish Druids to monks and scholars in Europe to kick start the European Renaissance. The Goddess-worshipping temples are thus the fountainhead of all modern Western knowledge, arts and sciences.

Lucius Apuleius was a Nubian-born scholar, writer, poet and Goddess-worshipper. He was the last great pagan, Goddess-worshipping philosopher. The great Greek-Egyptian scientist, librarian, music theorist, mathematician, astronomer, astrologer, and geographer Ptolemy may have been a Goddess-priest. The star charts of Ptolemy are the original source for all modern astronomy. Like Pythagoras Ptolemy thought that maths was the Divine revealed, not only an investigation of pure physics.

The fundamentals of modern science and maths developed out of the ancient Goddess temples, as did modern Western medicine, literature, music, dance, art, astrology and astronomy. But modern science lacks the inner or deeper search for truth as was found in the ancient Goddess temples. Modern science only looks at the surface of things, their form, structure and biological or physical function. It does not try to penetrate to any deeper or inner meaning, spiritual, religious, metaphysical or otherwise. Modern science merely observes and rationalises, failing to listen to the 'inner voice' and 'hush the unquiet mind.'

Chapter Nineteen

Modern Scientific Worship of 'Holy Mud'

Modern science is a kind of abstract idolatrous worship of materialism and money. Science accuses religion of bowing down to idols, to fictitious gods and superstition, but modern science bows down to 'Holy Mud', to the sticks and stones of the material world. Modern science has turned the material world (and the technology, money and machines which power science) into idols. Science worships the 'Holy Mud' of the material world, and only what human beings' limited intellect and senses can see, feel or quantify. Modern science has no internal vision. What can humans really know from just the material world? We live for an instant in a vast ocean of infinity and eternity, perhaps without beginning or end. What science has discovered about life is no more than the examination of a few pebbles on a beach beside a vast ocean of space and time, as Newton once said. How can humans know the meaning of it all (as science thinks it can discover) since we inhabit for the briefest of spans a tiny speck of dust in space called planet earth in a vast whirling vortex of time, matter, energy, and space? How can science quantify or qualify the whole of eternity, infinity, time and space? To do that we would need to be eternal and infinite, like a deity, but each human individual is imprisoned and limited by his or her body, his or her senses, his or her intellect, and his or her cultural norms of thought and being. All human beings are full of errors, change, emotions, hubris and partially revealed concepts, and that includes the ideas and theories of scientists.

Science is limited in the truths it can reveal, since human scientists themselves are limited in their knowledge and circumstances. Science can never be truly objective since it is a human invention and thus subject to culture, zeitgeist, errors, emotion, change and death. Scientific ideas and theories can be warped by success, money, privilege, and personal bias. Human knowledge and science constantly change as a result of new ideas, discoveries, and experiences. Nothing can have the final say, and that includes scientific knowledge.

Humans should never cease from exploring, studying and using everything at their disposal to acquire knowledge, and that includes exploring and studying science as well as philosophy, metaphysics, the occult and paranormal studies. Materialistic science looks down on metaphysics, the occult and the paranormal, but by doing so science resembles a frog at the bottom of a well limiting its vision to the small round hole at the top of the well showing an infinitesimal fraction of the sky above, and believing that it shows the whole of existence. There is so much more to existence than scientific knowledge, so many more things to be seen or experienced than the limited world view and viewpoint of materialistic science.

Materialistic science is basically a limited humanist philosophy of life. It worships man, his scientific knowledge and his technological achievements. This has been the case in both the capitalist states of the modern world and in the Communist states of the twentieth century. Orthodox Marxist Communism is atheistic, and in the Marxist-Communist states mere human beings came to be idolised as gods, such as the 'cult of personality' surrounding Lenin, Stalin, Mao, Marx and Engels, who were viewed as almost immortal emperor-gods or philosopher-kings. The Marxist Utopia came to be seen as a heaven on earth, not a heaven in the after-life. The proletariat came to be seen as a kind of angelic being fighting against the evil capitalist and bourgeois 'devils' to construct the materialistic Marxist Utopia on earth and in this life, not in the next. Even though Marxist Communism had an atheistic, materialistic and scientific philosophy of life, it was really an inversion of Christianity which returned in an inverse manner in Communist societies. Perhaps it is impossible to eradicate religious thought from the human soul or mind, which will return in a warped way even in purportedly atheistic societies.

In capitalist societies money has come to replace religion and religious ethics. Success is not necessarily based on hard work, fraternal love, honesty or peace since corrupt, ruthless, selfish, greedy, and exploitative business people, politicians, bankers, stockbrokers, lawyers and arms dealers do succeed, get rich, flourish and rise to the top of society. Money may not be able to necessarily buy you love or happiness but in a capitalist society it is 'enabling'. Money 'enables' everything for the individual in the capitalist society, for good or for ill. Little money limits everything for the individual, and brings discomfort and fear.

Chapter Twenty

Darwin's Capitalist, Competitive Theory of Evolution and Kropotkin's Communist, Co-operative Theory of Evolution

The Russian geographer, zoologist and anarchist-communist Kropotkin's co-operative theory of evolution is a valid alternative to Darwin's capitalist and competitive theory of evolution. Darwin's theory of evolution is really drawn not only from nature but from his own pre-conceived philosophy of life, based on White Anglo-Saxon Protestant and capitalist ideas. Darwin's theory is as much political and cultural as it is objective and biological. Its philosophy of life is based on ideas and observations based on nature as well as on Darwin's own cultural milieu, Victorian England with its capitalist socio-economic competition, its imperialism and its feudalism. These factors gave rise to Darwin's ideas about survival of the fittest and natural selection as much as his observations of nature, which were coloured by his philosophy of life and cultural milieu. Darwin's theory of evolution is partially based on the political tricks and philosophical chicanery used by Victorian capitalist society to keep the system in place, exploit labour and exploit nature. It thus promotes competition and mutual strife as opposed to co-operation and mutual aid in nature, whereas in nature co-operation is as much a common feature as struggle is in maintaining life, as Kropotkin wisely pointed out.

Natural selection is not always valid when it comes to survival in nature. In most natural disasters animals and plants do not survive or die based on their sexually competitive 'fitness', but deaths are random or absolute. Natural disasters do not pick out the sexually-competitively 'less fit' animals to destroy since everything is destroyed indiscriminately in earthquakes, tidal waves, floods, fires, volcanic explosions, etc. The sexually-competitively 'fit' are killed along with the 'less sexually-competitively fit.' Nature does not discriminate either intentionally or unintentionally or along any laws of nature or human theories about 'survival of the fittest.' Chance, luck and accident play as important a role as competition. In predation predators will eat any animal they can, not the less sexually-competitively fit, but any animal they chance across.

Evolution is just one tiny piece of the jigsaw of existence, and a very small and insignificant one at that. Existence is far more complex and subtle than Darwin's theory allows at the molecular, biological, psychological, emotional, planetary, solar and galactic levels. The universe is not held together by Darwin's little philosophy of life with its trivial little obsession with the passing on of genetic material and competition. Existence is so much more wonderful, subtle and complex than that!

Chapter Twenty-One

There is More to Life than the Scientific Concept of Reality

What is reality? A sunset or a rainbow can be viewed as a cascade of colours in the eyes of a painter, the refraction of light rays in the eyes of a physicist, a sign from the gods, an omen of good luck, a miracle, as a natural, supernatural, supra-natural, spiritual or aesthetic occurrence. It all depends on one's perception. The physicist's perception of reality is no less 'real' than the painter's or the miracle seeker's perception of reality. If God is higher than reason (mind) and matter then perhaps the scientific physicist's concept of reality is the lowest kind. If God creates things out of nothing, neither out of mind nor out of matter, then everything does not have to have a physical or material first cause. Reason, intellect and matter are just three aspects of Creation. They are not the only foundations of reality. Reason and intellect observe, describe and explain life, but perhaps the ultimate goal and purpose of nature (Creation) is not intellectual understanding or reason or Darwinism or chance or necessity or human logic but simply that the Divine Light shines throughout the world through good deeds and good thoughts.

The human brain is part of nature and human intelligence is thus limited to nature. Anything above or beyond nature is also above or beyond human understanding. We can only imperfectly know what truth is and what reality is. We can only ever receive imperfect knowledge of anything, and that includes a scientific understanding of anything. All ends in mystery! Science maintains that there is nothing higher (no explanation higher) than what can be derived from scientific understanding. But there is much more to life than the scientist's materialistic, biological or physical explanations. Science is a limited form of understanding which proceeds from the imperfect human brain and the imperfect human intellect which is subject to mistakes and ignorance. Scientific ideas and theories change and evolve over time so cannot form an everlasting truth, and the universe itself changes over time. Economic, technological and material forces themselves influence changes and developments in human society and thought. Material interests themselves clash among peoples, cultures and classes to influence human thought. Science, philosophy, and human thought change and morph constantly, so scientific thought is not more truthful than any other mode of thought. Darwin's ideas about evolution are just ideas and a philosophy of life which were influenced by Darwin's socio-cultural milieu as much as by his observations of nature. As Marx and Engels wrote, 'The ruling ideas of each age have ever been the ideas of its ruling class.'

Science cannot prove or disprove the existence of God or spirituality, not if it searched for a billion years. God is above the material world of the scientist. Science seeks proof in the material world of matter, in nature, in natural laws, in the limited human intellect. But God is above and beyond the reach of science, intellectualism, atoms, molecules, chemicals, biology, life, matter, planets, solar systems, galaxies and universes. God is everything and nothing, life and death, knowing and unknowing, everything in the known universe and beyond, and beyond that as well. The little intellects and the little egos of scientists can never grasp or understand or encompass the nature of God. Science can partially understand and control nature, but the nature of God or the Universal Will is much more than humans can ever understand. Science worships the 'Holy Mud' of matter and has transformed this mud of matter into a form of idolatry. Science worships the material world and the abstract laws of nature. Science cannot or will not or dare not examine such ideas as God, free will, evil, virtue, freedom, equality, fraternity, etc. Philosophy, religion and metaphysics enter the regions where science dare not follow.

Chapter Twenty-Two

Myths and Legends Concur with Science – Darwin Pre-Empted in Ancient Tibet

Myths and legends concur with science. They are scientific and metaphysical truths in the form of stories. Old Tibetan legends say that humans are descended from a monkey and an ogre. Early female hominids were probably frightful to look at with their sloping brows, prognathous jaws, large teeth, hairy bodies, big mouths, flat noses, jug ears, etc, and looked like apish ogresses. Early male hominids similarly resembled apes. This entirely concurs with Darwin's theory that humans are descended from apes. The Tibetans pre-empted Darwin by thousands of years. The Ancient Greek philosopher Anaximander thought that all living creatures arose from water, and that humans are descended from fish or fish-like animals. This also concurs with Darwin's theory. Hindu myths say that the universe is billions of years old and that the universe is continually created, sustained and then destroyed in a never-ending cycle. This myth concurs with modern science which also believes that the universe is billions of years old and was created at some point billions of years ago. Modern science believes it has discovered everything worth knowing, but people of all ages and all cultures possessed that knowledge in a different form.

Modern science lacks the ethical or metaphysical truths of the myths and legends of ancient times. It recognises only the 'Holy Mud' of matter and refuses to understand anything beyond that. But that is sheer blindness, folly and hubris on its part. It worships matter and seeks to conquer life through struggle against matter. This has led to the exploitation of nature, natural resources and animals on an unprecedented scale. But true scientific knowledge and love of everything should work hand-in-hand. True scientific knowledge and love should be indissoluble and form the real basis of life. As Einstein wrote, 'The most important function of science is to awaken the cosmic religious feeling and keep it alive.'

Chapter Twenty-Three

Astrophysics and the Big Bang Theory Pre-Empted by Medieval Spanish-Jewish Rabbi

The Spanish-Jewish rabbi, philosopher, physician and Cabbalist Nachmanides (1194-1270) pre-empted the theories of astrophysics by a thousand years. Nachmanides' commentary on the creation and expansion of the universe corresponds to what modern astrophysics believes – that the Big Bang occurred when a single point of matter expanded to form the universe. Nachmanides wrote:

'...At the briefest instant following creation all the matter of the universe was concentrated in a very small place, no larger than a grain of mustard. The matter at this time was very thin, so intangible, that it did not have real substance. It did have, however, a potential to gain substance and form and to become tangible matter. From the initial concentration of this intangible substance in its minute location, the substance expanded, expanding the universe as it did so. As the expansion progressed, a change in the substance occurred. This initially thin noncorporeal substance took on the tangible aspects of matter as we know it. From this initial act of creation, from this ethereally thin pseudosubstance, everything that has existed, or will ever exist, was, is, and will be formed.'

Everything that has existed, exists, or will exist proceeds from the divine point of eternity. This divine point of eternity sees the total reality. Time is an illusion, the inadequate ability of nature to contemplate eternity. Space is an illusion, the inadequate ability of nature to encompass everything, the one, the all. Humans thus see things as fragmented objects in moments of succession. Only the divine point of eternity, God, sees the universe as a complete entity unfolding in time as one total reality. Science can never have direct knowledge of this.

According to the Spanish-Jewish philosopher Solomon ibn Gabirol (c.1021-1058) the universe is composed of three 'substances'

– the first substance is Godhead, the second is matter and form, and the third is the will as intermediary between Godhead and matter/form. Solomon ibn Gabirol thought that God's existence is knowable, but not his being or his constitution since no attribute is predicable of God save that of existence. Religion examines the Godhead, science examines matter and form, and philosophy examines the will, which is the bridge or intermediary between Godhead (religion) and science (matter and form).

Chapter Twenty-Four

Miracle-Working Rabbi

There are many stories, rumours and opinions about Jesus' life, which are often contradictory. There is no proven contemporaneous documentation about Jesus, either Roman or Jewish. If we admit that Jesus existed, then we run into yet more obscurity. Was Jesus a magician who studied magic in Egypt, a miracle-working maverick Jewish rabbi, a charlatan, a holy man, the Son of God, the Messiah, or a Jewish heretic who dabbled in sorcery? Nothing can be proven about the real Jesus. Some sources put forward one perspective on his life and others the contrary. Some sources say he was a fraudster who was thrown out of yeshiva for his arrogance. They say he frequented prostitutes and that he was a severe-faced hunchbacked dwarf with scanty hair (not the blond-haired Aryan of the European imagination). Mary is reputed to have been a prostitute and an adulteress (hence the necessity of the Immaculate Conception). Jesus is said to have been the illegitimate son of the prostitute Mary and a Roman or Greek soldier called Panthera. Or perhaps Jesus was a beautiful, good and holy man who sacrificed his life for a just and ideal world. It is impossible to disentangle the lies from the truth about Jesus' life, the fictions from the facts. Was he really the one and only Son of God, since are not all human beings the Sons and the Daughters of God? Did Jesus appear on every planet in the universe to give them his message, and how can a mere mortal man be a God?

Jesus was a miracle-working Jewish rabbi who was able to evoke God's mercies and compassion on suffering humans. He could perform cures, and had mystical powers to foresee or interpret events and personalities. Miracle workers like Jesus have often appeared in Jewish history, for example, Moses. These miracle workers could 'override' nature and the laws of nature to perform God-like miracles. They understood the holiest four-letter name of God (the 'Tetragrammaton') which enabled them to perform supra-good miracles to help others. They used the Tetragrammaton during deep meditation by pronouncing it out loud or visualising it in their mind to work miracles. They are called 'Baal Shem' or 'Master of the Divine Name.' They could also use the names of angels in this magical way to work miracles. According to the Ancient Greek pagan philosopher Celsus (A.D. c170), Jesus was a magician who possessed a 'parhedros', a superhuman or divine assistant who could bring forth nourishment and organize banquets including such things as water, wine, bread, oil and vinegar.

Jesus was born Jewish, lived Jewish and died Jewish. He spoke the Jewish Psalms at his death. He was a righteous, holy man or 'tsaddik' from Galilee, a Jewish 'shaman' who could perform miracles. Galilee during Jesus' lifetime was full of holy men and prophets, such as John the Baptist, who could perform miracles and prophesy. Jesus was a Jewish prophet, healer, teacher and unofficial rabbi who combined his Jewish upbringing with Indian Buddhist doctrines (there had been Buddhist proselytisers in the Middle East for many generations before Christ), Chaldean and Egyptian magic. Later on Jesus' teachings became impregnated with the ideas of later Christian thinkers such as Saint Paul, who rejected the Jewish Jesus of the Jerusalem Jews and made Jesus' teachings universally applicable to Jews and non-Jews alike. Jesus became not only the Messiah of the Jews but also a universal Messiah for all humankind. Jesus' teachings were diluted with Mithraism and paganism. Mithras was a pre-Christian sun god who died and was resurrected. In the pagan Roman Virgil's Fourth Eclogue (Virgil died 19 years before Christ's birth) there is mentioned a chaste, Virgin Lady whose son will usher in a Golden Race and world peace.

Chapter Twenty-Five

The World's Greatest Scientist was also a Philosopher, Alchemist and Theologian

Isaac Newton studied not only physics, mechanics, optics, astronomy, maths, the nature of light, and gravitation but also philosophy, alchemy, Hermeticism and religion. In fact, Newton wrote more on religion than on science. Newton possessed one of the finest alchemical libraries in the world. Newton during his lifetime was accused of being a Rosicrucian, which may or may not be true. Newton learnt Hebrew to study the secret wisdom of the Bible and said he wanted to know the mind of God. He believed that the floor plan of Solomon's Temple was a cryptogram of the entire universe. He thought that the law of gravitation had been fully understood in ancient times and that Moses was an alchemist and a scientist who knew about atoms and gravity. It has been said that Moses learnt (from the Ancient Egyptians) arithmetic, geometry, metre, harmony, rhythm, symbolism, holy inscriptions, Assyrian letters, Chaldean astrology and astronomy, magic, necromancy, divining and other occult lore. Moses was the adopted Hebrew son of the Egyptian royal family. He grew up to be a famous Egyptian priest and magician. At the age of 40, he left Egyptian court life to help the Hebrews, his own people. Newton thought that the Ancient Egyptians possessed an advanced and secret science, and that the holders of this knowledge in Ancient Egypt knew that the earth orbited the sun along with the other planets, that the earth turned on its axis, and that the sun remained at rest. Copernicus said that he arrived at his insights by studying the secret writings of the Egyptians. The seventeenth-century mathematician Kepler said he stole ideas from the Egyptians to formulate his own laws of planetary orbits.

Chapter Twenty-Six

Divine Reflexes and God's Thoughts

Belief in angels might appear to be silly or childish to rationally or scientifically minded people. But we should not forget that many world-famous people from all walks of life (scientists, artists, poets, musicians, politicians, mystics, prophets, mathematicians, philosophers, chemists, psychics, physicists, etc) have seen, experienced or had visions of angels. William Blake saw angels, ghosts and spirits. George Washington had a vision of an angel which foretold the future history of America to him. Marc Chagall saw a blue angel. Joan of Arc had clairaudience of angels. Emanuel Swedenborg conversed with angels and spirits, and was taken to heaven many times. Swedenborg developed the nebula idea of galaxies. Handel heard angelic voices. Saint Francis of Assisi saw and heard an angel playing a violin. Mohammed and Abraham had visions of angels. J.R.R. Tolkien had clairaudience of an angel. Joseph Smith conversed with an angel called Moroni. Descartes received his 'rational' philosophy from an angel in a dream. Moses saw an angel in a burning bush. John Dee talked with angels. Edward Kelly channelled a complex series of magical letters which he believed was the language of angels. William Lilly heard angels speak. The nineteenth-century chemist Friedrich Kekule discovered the formula for benzene from a vision of a snake devouring its own tail (an angelic message perhaps). Georg Cantor experienced visions of God and angels, which he 'converted' into mathematical formulae. These formulae were later developed into number theory, 'absolute zero' and 'absolute infinity' concepts by Cantor. The seventeenth-century mathematician and physicist Blaise Pascal had mystical visions (perhaps angelic guidance). Dante, Charles Lindbergh, John Donne, Origen, John Milton, Thomas Aquinas, Martin Luther King, Tagore, Jung, Saint Augustine, Emerson and Edward Young all believed in, experienced, or had visions of angels. Perhaps there is more than mere myth or superstition to the existence of angels.

The French writer Villiers de l'Isle-Adam wrote that angels are '...spirits which the Unrevealed uttered outside time and days. Externalised effluvia of divine Necessity, the Angels exist, in substance, only in the sublime freedom of the absolute Heavens, where reality is united with the Ideal. They are thoughts of God's, discontinued as separate beings by the effect of omnipotence. Divine reflexes, they are manifest only in the ecstasy which they arouse and which forms part of Themselves.' (*Cruel Tales,* 1883)

The English writer Daniel Defoe believed implicitly in angels, but denied the existence of ghosts, fairies and hobgoblins. Defoe thought that angels existed but that other supernatural beings were childish and ignorant superstitions. Defoe believed that God contacted man directly through the medium of angels, and that the angels' main means of communication with man was through dreams. The angels' main function was to warn and advise man since Defoe contended that 'From whence else come all those private notices, strong impulses, pressings of spirit, involuntary joy, sadness and foreboding apprehensions and the like, of, and about things immediately and really attending us, and this in the most momentous articles of our lives.' Defoe said that he himself '...had never any considerable mischief or disaster attending me, but sleeping or waking I have had notice of it before-hand, and had I listened to these notices, I believe might have shunned the evil...' But Defoe did not believe that all dreams were due to angelic ministration, but accepted that the imagination could conjure up any fancy or trifle in the human mind. Defoe thought that the Devil (a Fallen Angel) had hosts of angels ready to tempt man in his dreams.

Perhaps angels exist or perhaps they do not, perhaps they are figments of our imagination or our subconscious mind, but whatever they are, real or imaginary or subconscious thoughts, they have played a crucial role in artistic and scientific discoveries and ideas, and always a positive role.

'The angels keep their ancient places;
Turn but a stone, and start a wing!
Tis ye, tis your estranged faces,
That miss the many-splendoured thing.'
(Francis Thompson, *The Kingdom of God*)

Chapter Twenty-Seven

Higher or Cosmic consciousness

Humankind has barely even begun to explore consciousness. We are surrounded by a creative matrix of eternity and infinity which we hardly understand. Humankind is much more than a breathing, eating and reproducing creature of materialist science. We have been given a soul and a mind to master our own destiny. If we would try to reach out and understand we could, as William Blake believed, open and cleanse the doors of perception so that everything would appear as it is, infinite. We must use all of our understanding, action, inquisitiveness and contemplation to ponder space, time, force, matter, the universal whole and higher realities. But today the shallow illusion of matter and corporeality hides and stains the white radiance of eternity from our eyes, as Shelley believed.

In modern secular society functions have been confused with goals. Capitalisation, competition, consumerism and desire become goals in themselves and drive human behaviour. Yet they are merely functions, like the need to gain warmth, shelter, food, clothing, etc, not the ultimate goals of human evolution which is for understanding, mind expansion, soul growth and knowledge. Anyhow, should we not be trying to escape from the prison of our limited corporeality and desires which can be achieved through the imagination, the mind and the spirit? We must explore the meaning of everything unlimited by the walls, boundaries and borders of materialist science and organised religions. They cannot hold back humankind's creative evolution which will continue until the final end of the universe or until humankind itself dies out, if the universe can ever end or if humankind does have an end. Perhaps the universe has no fixed beginning and no ultimate end, but is infinite and eternal, and un-bounded by time or space. All ends in mystery.

Secular society has forgotten the concepts of wisdom, spirituality, and creative evolution. It has denied the sacredness of humanity and can provide no guiding principle of how to live. It has sunk into the abyss of materialism and money-driven goals, concepts, tasks and values. Secular science can partly explain the physical universe in materialist terms, but human beings are not only creatures of reason obeying laws of logic, but also beings of creative imperfection opening towards infinity. Behind our impermanent corporeality, intellect and personality there is also a soul, a higher self, a genius, a guiding angel, or internal guru. Science believes that life and consciousness arose out of matter, but perhaps matter arose out of life and consciousness. That idea really turns the tables on secular science and materialism. Life is not a random, meaningless, biological accident if life and consciousness is put before matter. Science says that the true reality is to be discovered in the physical and sensory world and all else is fancy, chimerical, inane, imagination, illusion, delusion, myth or fairy tale. But seeing, touching, hearing, smelling, tasting, measuring, intellectualising, and rationalising something is only a distillation of reality. Reality is wider, deeper, larger and more complex than to be found in the minute brain, body or senses of a human being, or through his artificial machines, tools, scientific instruments and logical theories.

Humans are intuitive as well as logical, and mystical as well as rational, creatures who see inwardly as well as outwardly. Inner knowing is as important as the external authority of science, organised religion, politics, socio-economic structures, the laws of nature, material reality and reason. Science, reason, reductionism and determinism cannot explain or explore everything that exists in this vast, mysterious, creative universe. Only a religious or a scientific hubris believes it can. Secularism, scientific dualism, materialism and reductionism have privileged matter and body over mind and spirit, sanctified materialistic consumerism, and the chaos of the free market over socio-economic co-operation. But how can such beliefs create a world of health, beauty and spirit? Humankind can evolve further. Nothing is fixed forever and if evolution is true, then it in its turn should evolve over time into a more complex form or idea, as living species do.

Some of the philosophical ideas underpinning Darwin's theory of evolution seem a little suspect. Nature is not always and at all times cruel, brutal and ruthless. The Russian evolutionist and philosopher Kropotkin pointed this out long ago and showed that nature is also often selfless, kind, protective, loving, co-operative and trusting.

There is a harmony in nature, not only ruthless competition and survival of the fittest. Nature is also too complex to be explained in terms of accident. It seems to have a purpose beyond the passing on of genetic material, a creative purpose beyond the matter it is composed of. Darwin's theory views life as awful, woeful and heartless, which seems to me to reflect the emergence of ruthless capitalism in nineteenth-century England, which Darwin must have witnessed in his lifetime. He transferred through his theory of evolution this emerging competitive capitalist society to all of nature. The idea of evolution itself is bound by time and space, and perhaps evolution itself can evolve to a higher and better form, such as the Messianic Age of Isaiah.

I think the writer and philosopher Olaf Stapledon (1886-1950) had a far deeper and holistic understanding of the history, origin, shape, evolution and possible futurity of the universe than the received wisdom of modern, conventional, secular science or revealed religion. Stapledon saw the universe as expanding into an infinite number of Creations or universes. He saw time as cyclical and never-ending, and time and space as revolving or radiating around the 'viewpoint of eternity', which lives through and apprehends all things and all at once. This can be envisaged or illustrated in diagrammatical form.[3] The nature or mystery of the 'viewpoint of eternity' humankind on earth partly divines as a search for God. God could be the lord of the universe, an outlaw, almighty or crucified, power itself, wisdom, law, righteousness, love, 'not-love', worship, inhumanity, nothing at all, a self-subsistent nothing, pure reason, the divine mathematician, some inhuman spirit, an exquisite creature of humankind's mind, unreasoning creativity, the darkness upon the throne, the truth, the star maker, the supreme artist, all of these things, or none of these things. But whatever it is 'our hearts praise it, out-soaring reason' (Olaf Stapledon, *Starmaker*). Or perhaps the Cosmos just 'is', and the idea of function or purpose in relation to the Cosmos is meaningless.

The narrator of Stapledon's novel *Starmaker* travels through time and space as a 'disembodied, wandering viewpoint'. He meets all kinds of human and non-human intelligences throughout the universe including super-intelligent beings evolved from slug-like creatures, insects, plants, crustaceans, fish, echinoderms, molluscs, nautiloids, birds, bird-clouds, communal intelligences of multi-organisms,

---

[3] See Illustration B

composite beings and quasi-men. Some intelligences have developed telepathy to a high degree and other intelligences have evolved different kinds of senses to perfection. They communicate through, for example, scent or taste, which underpins the whole philosophical, aesthetic, artistic, and scientific basis of their societies, as sight does in ours.

From high up in space the narrator of the novel sees the planet earth as a living being with the '...delicacy and brilliance, the intricacy and harmony of a live thing. Strange that in my remoteness I seemed to feel, as never before, the vital presence of Earth as of a creature alive but tranced and obscurely yearning to wake.' On the surface of planet earth teems humankind, who the narrator describes as '...world-mastering, self-torturing, incipiently angelic beasts.' The earth looked at from space becomes merely but gloriously a '...little round grain of rock and metal, filmed with water and with air, whirling in sunlight and darkness. And on the skin of that little grain all the swarms of men, generation by generation, had lived in labour and blindness, with intermittent joy and intermittent lucidity of spirit. And all their history, with its folk-wanderings, its empires, its philosophies, its proud sciences, its social relations, its increasing hunger for community, was but a flicker in one day of the lives of stars.'

The narrator of the novel proposes that the stars and even whole galaxies might in some way be 'alive' and conscious. The movement of the stars seems to the narrator to be vital and questing, as if they are living creatures taking cognizance of one another from afar, then uniting to form binaries, or swinging hyperbolically around one another and then away from each other. He views the stars as more than mere 'fire-balls' which are just whirling and travelling according to the geometrical laws of their most minute particles. The whole galaxy appears to the narrator as a '...great and lovely creature...' which '...must be alive, must have intelligent experience of itself and of things other than it.' The galaxy appears to behave like a living organism, with its '...delicate tracery of star-streams, like the streams within a living cell; and its extended wreaths, almost like feelers; and its nucleus of light.' Perhaps the stars and even the whole galaxy itself are more than just a 'waste of fire' but somehow alive.

The stars are psychologically and physiologically very different from other living organisms. A star can perceive its cosmic environment and its position in relation to other stars. A star's life consists of a kind of dance through space to achieve in its motion a blissful, ecstatic and an ever more successful pursuit of formal beauty. Stars not only have a life of physical movement but also a cultural and spiritual life. Each star is aware of its fellow stars as conscious beings, and this mutual awareness is intuitive and telepathic. All stars aim to perfectly execute their part in the galactic dance in relation to the other stars.

The narrator thinks there are several types of consciousness in the universe, namely, star consciousness; the minded world consciousness of living creatures on planets (such as of humankind and other forms of life on planet earth); galactic consciousness (between minded worlds within and between galaxies); and nebular consciousness (between nebulae). Then there is the ultimate, sublime, unknowable consciousness of the 'star maker', the source and goal of all nebulae, stars, living creatures on minded worlds and all finite things.

The star maker is the creative force and unity within, above, beyond, behind, beneath and incipient to the universe. It is known by many names and worshipped, or feared, as innumerable deities, or the infinity that humankind calls God, Nature, Evolution, the Macrocosm, the Great First Cause, the Big Bang, the Great Spirit, Yahweh, Love Consciousness, Christ Consciousness, Buddha Consciousness, the Great Mother, or the universe as an infinite and eternal 'Whole'.

The star maker has two aspects. Firstly, as a particular creative mode that has given life to everything (the whole Cosmos) and, secondly, as something incomparably greater than creativity, that is, as the eternally achieved perfection of the absolute spirit. The universe came about when the infinite and eternal spirit limited itself with finite and temporal being. It became self-limited for creativity, and objectified from itself an atom of its infinite potentiality. This atom was the microcosm or germ of a proper time and space, and all the kinds of cosmic beings. The matter of ten million galaxies lay dormant in a point. Then the 'Big Bang' occurred (as it states in Genesis, 'Let there be light') and the cosmos exploded into being, actualising its potentiality of space and time. Light leaped and blazed. The centres of power, like fragments of a bursting bomb, were hurled apart. But each one retained in itself, as a memory and a longing, the single spirit of the whole, and each mirrored in itself aspects of all the others throughout all cosmic space and time. No longer punctual (in a point), the cosmos became a volume of inconceivably dense matter and inconceivably violent radiation, constantly expanding. The congested and exploding cloud of fire swelled until it was of a planet's size, a star's size, the size of a whole galaxy, and of ten million galaxies. And in swelling it became more tenuous, less brilliant, and less turbulent. Presently the cosmic cloud was disrupted by the stress of its expansion in conflict with the mutual clinging of its parts, and was disrupted into many million cloudlets, the swarm of the great nebulae. More and more rapidly the nebulae retreated from one another, and at the same time each nebular cloud contracted, becoming first like a ball of down and then like a spinning lens and then a featured whirl of star-streams. Still the cosmos expanded, until the galaxies that were most remote from one another were flying apart so swiftly that the creeping light of the cosmos could no longer bridge the gulf between them. As far as the future is concerned the cosmos will keep on expanding until the last galaxy dies and then complete physical quiescence will reign.

Or perhaps all of the above is a myth, a dream, a faint echo of the truth or reality and, 'Peering, the mind could see nothing sure, nothing in all human experience to be grasped as certain, except uncertainty itself; nothing but obscurity gendered by a thick haze of theories. Man's science was a mere mist of numbers; his philosophy but a fog of words. His very perception of this rocky grain and all its wonders was but a shifting and a lying apparition. Even oneself, that seeming-central fact, was a mere phantom, so deceptive, that the most honest of men must question his own honesty, so insubstantial that he must even doubt his very existence. And our loyalties! so self-deceiving, so misinformed and misconceived. So savagely pursued and hate-warped! Our very loves, and these in full and generous intimacy, must be condemned as unseeing, self-regarding, and self-congratulatory.' (Stapledon, *Starmaker*) Yet, as Stapledon believes, above all of this obscurity and uncertainty, the hope of a saner, a more reasonable, a more conscious and a happier world.

The immensity, obscurity and uncertainty of life and the cosmos opens up such terrifying vistas of reality that one wishes to retreat to the false but comforting securities of a new Dark Age, to paraphrase H.P. Lovecraft. For example, if Wales represented just the size of our own galaxy (say 100,000 light years across) then planet Earth is reduced to a grain one-twentieth of an inch across. However, the physical immensity of the universe is also a comforting thought, since within that immensity on the hundreds of thousands of millions of billions of worlds there must also surely be a myriad of rich, diverse and complex life, whether nebular, stellar, planetary or galactic.

Chapter Twenty-Eight

Revolution in Thought and Perception

What the world needs now is a new cultural, spiritual and artistic revolution to shake off the dust of secular, scientific cosmic pessimism, the dogma of revealed, organised religion, and conformity to capitalistic, money-driven values, tasks, and goals. They have been casting a shadow on the human spirit and a shroud over the earth for too long. Such a revolution in thought is possible, and since we are on the cusp of a new epoch, a new century, a new millennium, then it must surely come. Such cultural revolutions in thought have occurred in the past, such as during the Renaissance in Italy; during the 'Golden Age' of Moorish and Jewish Spain; during the Romantic Movement of the late eighteenth and early nineteenth centuries; and in the 1960s (in England, France, America, China and Russia). People need to develop their true potentiality of mind (free from scientific or religious dogma), to have spiritual experiences, skilled work, true interpersonal intercourse (not via the mass media or gadgets), and to devote some of their time to literature, music, the arts, inspired science, and the study or apprehension of nature. But today we would rather devote our time to consumerism, economic competition, business, marketing, entertainment, 'getting and spending', etc. And certain historians have called the modern world the 'end of history', supposedly being the greatest or the brightest expression of humankind's potentiality. The modern world is not the end of history, but a blip in the cosmic whole, and perhaps may prove to be the beginning of decay if we do not change our world or cosmic view. It may prove to be the decay of humankind's mental, spiritual, emotional, social and artistic self, and far from evolving into higher, brighter, more creative, better beings we might all be evolving metaphorically into 'perambulating grey blobs' (Chekhov).

The universe is not just a blind, groping, chaotic, meaningless vortex of matter, or a dead vacuum, or a spiritless machine, but a 'many-splendoured' thing of beauty, wonder, awe, infinity, creativity, heart, soul, and purpose. Everything is holy, or declined from holiness and groping towards the light. Everything is in a state of growth or development, animate and inanimate, destructive and creative, good and bad, sweet and bitter. We are surrounded by wonders and mysteries beyond our conception, and we must cleanse our organs of perception to see, and what we will see is things as they are, infinite, as Blake perceived. Cleansing the organs too much or too fast will lead to madness since our minds are unable to perceive infinity directly (as in drug-induced hallucinations), but cleanse them we must occasionally and a little, to let in the light of wonder, awe and creativity. And then we may perceive a heaven in a wild flower, a world in a grain of sand, infinity in the palm of our hand, eternity in an hour, books in brooks and sermons in stones, as Blake and Wordsworth perceived. We must occasionally lift our souls '...above this little earth, this folly-fettered world...' as the English poet Warton advised, in order to see the cosmic whole.

As well as looking outward we must also look inward to the unexplored regions of the mind, the internal or subconscious universe, and find eternity, infinity and God in the centre of our being, in the centre of every atom. As Henry David Thoreau advised in his book *Walden*, 'Direct your eye right inward and you'll find a thousand regions in your mind yet undiscovered. Travel them and be expert in home cosmography...'

Edgar Allen Poe in his essay *The Poetic Principle* believed the world of the mind can be divided into three modes of perception – Pure Intellect, Taste and Moral Sense. The Pure Intellect or Reason seeks truth and expediency. Taste seeks the beautiful or an elevated sense of perception, which Poe describes as 'the intoxication of the Heart.' This is the poetic intellect. Moral Sense is concerned with duty, conscience and obligation. Truth satisfies the reason. Poetry excites or elevates the soul. Passion excites the heart.

Scientific reason or intellect working alone is insufficient as far as our moral sense and poetic intellect are concerned. Science cannot sufficiently excite or elevate the soul and is inherently devoid of moral sense. Without moral sense and poetic intellect science is a barren search for truth and expediency on a material level. Science working alone is an inadequate and partial mode of perception. Science will only ever understand or perceive a part of reality.

Human beings are not only rational, logical, empirical, natural beings composed of matter, but also imaginative, intuitive, supernatural agencies of Ideality (the sense of the beautiful, the sublime, the mystical, spirituality and poetic yearnings). The poet and the artist are able to unite the rational mind and the visionary/contemplative imagination to produce music, poetry, art and beauty, to give insights into nature, and to see worlds beyond this world via the subconscious mind.

Science is able to name the stars and the elements, chart the seas and the skies, but it cannot measure the mind, or death. Science only explores earthly, mortal values and insights, and cannot grasp spiritual concerns. Science is only able to construct a matter-bound Earthly City and is unable to build a City of God or spirituality. Science pretends to see things objectively or neutrally but in reality it pushes an ideological or partial line. Science is neither infallibly true nor eternal, but is culturally contrived, subjective and ideological. Modern scientific ideals and so-called truths are bound up with technocratic, competitive, commercial, urban-industrial civilisations, since modern science propounds Darwin's ideas about evolution and not Kropotkin's (Social Darwinism over communitarianism), action is emphasised above contemplation, empiricism is valued over intuition, reason valued above imagination, material progress and change above stability and simplicity, etc. Science, like religion, wishes to impose its truths on reality and on nature, but nature and reality are ever-expansive and above humankind's laws, theories and intellect.

Science regiments thought and feeling on empirical lines. But the vanity and hubris of science is as nothing compared to the eternity of nature and death. As the poet Andrew Marvell reminds us,

'At my back I always hear
Time's winged chariot hurrying near;
And yonder all before us lie
Deserts of vast eternity.'

Thoreau believed that '...the art of life is to prepare ourselves, and to help others to prepare, to receive our portion of the Infinite.' William Blake called this portion of the Infinite which we can receive 'Fourfold Vision.' Fourfold Vision occurs when God, Man and the Universe become one. The mechanistic, materialistic Newtonian outlook of science is Single Vision, which Blake sees as a kind of spiritual blindness. Twofold Vision occurs when you see not of the eye, but through the eye, to perceive the spiritual reality behind the material world. Threefold Vision is when the subconscious mind becomes a source for creative art, visions and dreams. These four modes of perception are found in every human. Blake believed that Reason, which gives Single Vision, is the fallen part of the Divine Substance.

Reason and science keep humankind like blindfolded prisoners in the spiritual blindness of Single Vision, which Plato saw as a cave of shadows. But art and philosophy can release us from the cave of shadows. When you first leave the cave you are blinded by the light of Twofold, Threefold and Fourfold Vision. But your eyes gradually become accustomed to the light and you see objects, not shadows of objects. But go out of the cave into the light you must if you want to escape from spiritual blindness and imprisonment in the world of matter and shadows. But when you return to the cave to tell the prisoners there (the scientists, materialists, sceptics and cynics) who are living in a darkened world of illusion they will disbelieve and mock you, and say you are mad, foolish, unrealistic, idealistic or delusional. But this has always been the fate for artists, poets and philosophers! As Edgar Allen Poe wrote in his poem *Alone*,

'From childhood's hour I have not been
As others were – I have not seen
As others saw – I could not bring
My passions from a common spring.'

Philosophy and art search further than science allows itself. Science is only allowed to examine 'Second Causes', and hardly concerns itself with the Great First Cause, Least Understood. Science is content to admit the Big Bang or Act of Creation or Great First Cause occurred, but thinks it is worthless (because un-provable in an empirical/scientific/materialistic sense) to examine why, how and what existed before the Big Bang or Act of Creation. If science daren't or won't examine this, then it is up to art, philosophy and theology to do so, because what else will?

Agrippa said that physics teaches the nature of things, and mathematics their dimensions and extent, as well as calculating the movement of the heavenly bodies. But theology (and I would also add art and philosophy) can comprehend God (the Great First Cause), angels, demons, intelligence, soul, thought and the archetypal world. Art, philosophy and theology can examine the nature of the Great First Cause, the Godhead, and go to places and modes of perception where science dare not follow. It can seek God as an external force or as an 'inner light' which rises in humankind from the inside (as George Fox, the founder of the Quakers, believed). But science would reply that God and spirituality are un-provable and therefore delusional or non-existent, and by ousting God and spirituality from the universe freedom and enlightenment and the true nature of reality will ensue. However, in Dostoevsky's novel *The Devils* the death of belief in God does not lead to freedom and enlightenment but to a world reduced to boredom and meaninglessness. Even if God is proved to be not 'out there' in the external universe, that does not preclude levels of consciousness and planes of existence so deep inside the mind that the scientific intellect cannot conceive of, and dare not follow. Here, madness, sin, chaos and horror reign, as well as beauty, truth, love and harmony.

By uniting science with spirituality we will see that the universe is one great self-regulating organism, and that the human mind and will are parts of the universal whole. As the English poet Alexander Pope wrote in his poem *An Essay on Man*,

'All are but parts of one stupendous whole,
Whose body nature is, and God the soul...'

We must cleanse the organs of perception of our spiritual selves in order to,
'...open the Eternal Worlds, to open the immortal Eyes
Of man inwards into the Worlds of Thought, into Eternity
Ever expanding into the Bosom of God, the Human Imagination.'

(William Blake)

Chapter Twenty-Nine

Mis-shaping the Beauteous Forms of Things

'Improvement makes Straight Roads, but the Crooked Roads without Improvement are Roads to Genius.' (William Blake)

'The Tree which moves some to tears of joy is in the Eyes of others only a Green Thing that stands in the way.' (William Blake, 1799)

Materialistic, reductionist natural science has pauperised our apprehension of nature. Natural science seeks to apprehend nature in purely materialistic and rational terms. Nature is 'objectified' and dispassionately categorised, probed, dissected, rationalised, and compartmentalised, whether living or dead, individual or collective, internal or external. But there are other ways to understand, apprehend and 'know' nature. As Wordsworth wrote, 'Our meddling intellects mis-shape the beauteous forms of things; We murder to dissect.'

Not only by over-rationalisation but also by scientific progress and technological advancements large areas of the planet have been depleted of their natural fauna and flora. Modern techno-industrial society has had a devastating effect on wildlife and has urbanised a large portion of humankind. In the modern world with so much sophisticated technology at our disposal, amazing medical and surgical advancements to heal and extend life, a thousand domestic appliances and sciences for our ease and comfort, rapid international communications, spectacular entertainments, mass urbanisation, suburbanisation, air conditioned indoor and office life, and so on, we might forget (in our headlong rush for speed, modernity, efficiency, change and progress) any reverence for nature and animals. We might come to view the natural world as something unnecessary, meaningless and irrelevant to modern living, or economically unproductive, yet I believe concern, and indeed reverence, for nature is something eternal in the soul of man, vitally important and necessary for humankind's ongoing survival and happiness, and can be found in every culture or society throughout history and pre-history, regardless of that society's economic system, prosperity, or level of technological development. For example, in the wonderful and sublime nature poetry of Ancient Celtic and Gaelic Ireland; in the writings of the Russian scientist and anarchist Prince Peter Kropotkin in Tsarist and Communist Russia, who proposed a more co-operative Theory of Evolution than the competitive and pro-capitalistic leanings of Social Darwinism; in the poems and works of the English Romantic poets of the early nineteenth century, who called for a return to nature and the imagination; and in the teachings of the Hebrew prophet Moses, who proposed animal rights over two thousand years ago.

Indeed, Jewish culture has always recognised, worshipped and celebrated God's Creation, Nature, alongside the worship of its Creator. Psalm 148: 9-10 says, 'Praise him, hills and mountains, fruit-trees and forests; all animals, tame and wild, reptiles and birds.' Psalm 96: 11-13 says, 'Be glad, earth and sky! Roar, sea, and every creature in you; be glad, fields, and everything in you! The trees in the woods will shout for joy when the lord comes to rule the earth. He will rule the peoples of the world with justice and fairness.' In Job 38-41 the Lord shows his love and concern for wild animals such as lion cubs, raven chicks, and wild donkeys, as well as revealing the beauty, strength and wonder of animals, such as the Behemoth (hippopotamus), the ostrich, the horse and the eagle.

The Ancient Hebrews proposed animal rights and practised animal welfare millennia ago. Biblical injunctions for the protection of animals include Exodus 20: 10; 23: 4; 23: 5; and 23: 12, and Deuteronomy 5: 14; 22: 4; 22: 6-7; 22: 10; and 25: 4. Proverbs 12: 10 says, 'A good man takes care of his animals, but wicked men are cruel to theirs.' Moses and David were chosen to lead Israel partly because of their kindness to animals (according to the Midrash). The Talmud states, '[relieving] the suffering of an animal is a biblical law' (za'ar ba'alei hayyim de-oraita). The Talmud (Avodah Zarah 186) forbids hunting and gladiatorial shows for observant Jews. Nature conservation and soil preservation are commanded in the Tanakh (Hebrew Bible). Deuteronomy 20: 19-20 says, 'When you besiege a city...You shall not destroy its trees. You may cut from them but not destroy them.' Leviticus 25: 4 commands that agricultural land should be left to lie fallow every seventh year ('...a year of complete rest for the land...'), a commandment that modern-day factory farming practices should pay attention to, with the exhaustion and poisoning of the land today with chemical fertilisers. Hassidic teachings are markedly pantheistic, holding that divinity can be found everywhere, including in God's Creation, Nature.

So, reverence for nature, animal welfare and nature conservation is an ancient, primitive practice as well as a modern concern which, with so much power of destruction as well as creation in humankind's hands as never before, is vitally necessary if humankind is to get back in balance with the earth upon which everybody lives, and the beautiful wild which can provide us all with so much artistic, poetic, recreational, inspirational, medicinal, and spiritual benefits.

In the immortal words of Albert Einstein, 'The most beautiful and profound emotion that we can experience is the sensation of the mystical. It is the sower of all true science. He to whom this emotion is a stranger, who can no longer wonder and stand rapt in awe, is as good as dead... Our task must be to free ourselves...by widening our circle of compassion to embrace all living creatures, and the whole [of] nature in its beauty'.

Chapter Thirty

'Getting and Spending'

The predominant concept of history and time in the Western world is founded upon a mythical ideal, a mythical ideal of historical and universal 'progress'. This 'myth of progress' is linear as opposed to cyclical in its concept of time, since it postulates a linear, chronological, clockwork time or history created by machines, clocks and calendars, that is, by the human intellect. It is forward-looking and strenuously materialistic, since it predicts a rosy vision of an artificial technological utopia, and a technological utopia that is manipulative and exploitative of both natural as well as human 'resources', and directed towards selfish individualism and egoism.

The Western world values economic consumption, efficiency, material progress, individuality, commercial self-gain, and consumerism as the primary human or societal concerns. We are actively encouraged, and indeed rewarded, to strive and compete with each other to gain for ourselves perpetually bigger or better cars, domestic appliances, gadgets, exotic foodstuffs and holidays. Values such as sustainability, simplicity, asceticism, moderation, and asceticism are cynically sidelined, or conveniently ignored altogether. We are artificially encouraged, through clever advertising and marketing, to desire an easier, lazier, faster, push-button lifestyle, even though it is abundantly clear that that lifestyle not only threatens the very world which we all inhabit, but is also founded upon the exploitation of both our fellow man and the natural world. Yet in our consumer societies such exploitation, competition, artificiality, individualism, egoism, Mammonism, cynicism, selfishness, and destruction are not only desirable, but indeed necessary, to keep the wheels of our techno-industrial 'supply-and-demand' complex rolling forwards. However, it would be absurd to think we can now go back, or somehow 'return to nature', our 'dear, old, beautiful mother' (in the words of W.H. Hudson), since science and technology have given humankind so many comforts, freedoms and luxuries which it would be downright crazy and senseless to give up. Indeed, who would want to return to a completely 'natural' or 'primitive' way-of-life, with its harshness and circumscribed living conditions, and do without the Western world's sciences, appliances and communications for our day-to-day comfort and convenience?

It would be wilfully blinkered to deny the hugely beneficial and life-enhancing effects of science, commerce and technology for humankind (material, medical, agricultural, industrial, etc), yet it would also be wilfully cynical to dismiss the havoc and harm which such 'progress' has carelessly, unwittingly or uncaringly brought in its wake. Science, technology, and 'progress' on the material plane, and '-isms and -ologies' on the intellectual plane, should not be the supreme goals or 'deities' we should be devoting our best time and effort towards, but also nature, art, imagination, poetry, and our 'soul-life'. How foolishly people waste their lives 'getting and spending' and toil away their hours trying to maintain their decadent lifestyles (indeed they '...crave the right to toil'!). Two centuries ago right at the beginning of our modern, scientific, Western, industrialised, materialistic and urbanised era, the poet Wordsworth wisely said,

'The world is too much with us; late and soon,
Getting and spending, we lay waste our powers:
Little we see in nature that is ours;
We have given our hearts away, a sordid boon!
This sea that bares her bosom to the moon;
The winds that will be howling at all hours,
And are up-gathered now like sleeping flowers
For this, for everything, we are out of tune;
It moves us not...'

Is the planet earth and its bountiful nature to be only regarded in a scientific, economic, or utilitarian way, as just a natural 'resource', a tourist 'site', a recreational 'facility', an ecological 'store-house', or a genetic 'bank'? Are we modern Westerners really so blind and shallow that we cannot comprehend and invest nature with other qualities and values, rather than materialistic, economic, intellectual and utilitarian ones? Can nature not also provide humankind with spiritual, aesthetic, and inspirational discoveries and feelings? And how could humankind be happier, healthier and wiser if we continue to develop, or cultivate off the face of the earth, all of wild nature merely in our eagerness for material self-gain? And when we stand alone in a barren, chemically-sprayed landscape, a monocultural 'green desert', or a sprawling, traffic-choked metropolis does not the other side of unlimited and unchecked 'progress' reveal itself? Nor can the beauty and complexity of the universe be explained away by mere '-isms and -ologies', by scientific and reductionist left-hand brain thinking, since it really does not matter if you believe the world is flat, spherical, oblong, disc-shaped (as in Ancient Greece), or floating on the back of a turtle (as in Native North American myths), if there is no love, compassion, reverence, or true spiritual appreciation. As Wordsworth also said two centuries ago,

'Great God! I'd rather be
A pagan suckled in a creed outworn;
So might I, standing on this pleasant lea,
Have glimpses that would make me less forlorn;
Have sight of Proteus rising from the sea;
Or hear old Triton blow his wreathed horn.'

And as Saint Francis of Assisi sang eight centuries ago in his *Canticle to All Creation*:

'Praised be my Lord for our sister, Mother Earth, for she sustains and keeps us and brings forth all kinds of fruits together with grasses and bright flowers.'

Scientific discoveries and technological inventions have undeniably enlarged humankind's intellectual understanding of the physical or the material world, but the application of these very discoveries have also often been at the expense of the diversity and beauty of the natural world, since 'our meddling intellects misshape the beauteous forms of things we murder to dissect.' (Wordsworth).

The mechanistic concept of the natural world as a kind of machine or computer, or only a set of physical and chemical reactions, is an entirely cynical, blinkered and manipulative world-view. The Ancient World appears to have had a far greater philosophical understanding of the universe as a living, rather than a mechanical, entity. To the Ancient World, the entire universe was a harmonious living entity, and the concept of Godhead corresponded to the unity of the universe, as explained by the Roman author Pliny the Elder two thousand years ago: 'The world and this expanse are properly held to be a deity, everlasting, boundless, an entity without a beginning and one that will never end...The world is sacred, eternal, boundless, self-contained, or, one should say, complete in itself, finite yet resembling the infinite, of all things certain yet resembling the uncertain, embracing in its grasp all things without and within. The world is the work of Nature and, at the same time, the embodiment of Nature herself... I think it is a sign of human weakness to try to find out the shape and form of God. Whatever God is – provided he does exist – and in whatever region he is, God is the complete embodiment of sense, sight, hearing, soul, mind, and of himself...God is man helping man.' (Pliny the Elder, *Natural History*). This extremely ancient, pantheistic concept envisioned the Godhead as the entire universe, both the Creator and the Creation, Nature personified. The Godhead was seen as the unifying force of the universe, as opposed to its opposite state, Chaos or disunity. The outer, visible, sensory universe was the 'macro-cosmos' but within humankind's soul there was also a 'micro-cosmos', an infinitesimal epitome of the entire macro-cosmos, holding within itself a divine or intuitive knowledge. Humankind's collective and individual soul was viewed as the mind of the mind, and freedom was the uninhibited expression of the divine soul, a dance of the divine mind.

In the Western world today we proudly proclaim our hard-won human rights, democratic systems, freedoms, liberties and pluralistic societies, but are we really as free as we like to think we are? Have we actually just exchanged the repressive social bonds of the Church and the landed aristocracy as existed until the eighteenth century, for those of the nation-state and big business? In the Middle Ages the Church and the landed aristocracy went to war over land and natural resources, which is really no different to the numerous wars being waged today by nation-states (allied to those who control the means of production, that is, 'big business') also for land and natural resources. In fact, our capacity today to inflict death and destruction against our enemies is infinitely more pernicious and deadly than it was in medieval times. Mass murder and mutilation has never been so easy and effortless to commit. No longer must we laboriously hack our enemy to death with heavy sword or axe, strenuously pull a bow-string, or forcefully hurl a spear or javelin, since now we can merely push a button or flick a switch and, as if by magic and from a great distance, dispatch, maim and mutilate dozens, hundreds, thousands, even millions of our enemies. We can lay mines, drop bombs by the thousand from the air, shoot missiles from hundreds of miles away (and perhaps even from space!), gas or burn or infect with chemical and biological weapons, and vaporise our enemies with nuclear and atomic bombs.

'Man finds a paradise, and leaves a desert,' which is as true in the modern world today as it was when the Roman author Pliny wrote that sentence two thousand years ago. And when, during the course of mankind's 'conquest' of both nature and his political enemies or economic rivals, the entire world has become poisoned, polluted, degraded of its natural resources, completely cultivated for farmland, urbanised and 'civilised', and the wild creatures corralled, contained in parks, or simply scattered to the four winds, will mankind really be happier, healthier and wiser?

> 'What is man without the beasts?
> If all the beasts were gone,
> Men would die from a great loneliness of spirit.
> Whatever happens to the beast, happens to man.
> The earth does not belong to man;
> Man belongs to the earth.
> This we know.
> All things are connected
> Like the blood which unites one family.
> Whatever befalls the earth,
> Befalls the sons of the earth.'

(Chief Seattle)

> 'Men say they know many things,
> But lo! They have taken wings, –
> The arts and sciences,
> And a thousand appliances;
> The wind that blows
> Is all that anybody knows.'

(Henry David Thoreau)

> 'I had a dream which was not all a dream...
> The world was void,
> The populous and the powerful was a lump,

Seasonless, herbless, treeless, manless, lifeless, –
A lump of death- a chaos of hard clay.
The rivers, lakes, and ocean all stood still,
And nothing stirr'd within their silent depths.'
(Lord Byron, *Darkness*)

Chapter Thirty-One

The Home of Humankind

As it is stated in the philosophies of the Ancient World there are four elements which compose the universe (earth, air, fire and water), four seasons (spring, summer, autumn and winter), four major divine physical entities (the earth, the sun, the moon and the sky), and four humours in humankind with their corresponding emotional qualities (blood which corresponds to air and sensation, choler which corresponds to fire and intuition, phlegm which corresponds to water and emotion, and melancholy which corresponds to earth and thought). These divine truths were well-known in the Ancient World, and Pliny describes how the four elements compose the universe: 'I observe that there is no doubt about there being four elements. The uppermost is fire, source of those eyes of the great army of blazing stars. The next element is a vapour which the Greeks and ourselves call by the same name, "air" …Suspended by its force the earth is balanced in the middle of space, together with the fourth element – its waters.' (Pliny the Elder, *Natural History*)

As far as the seasons are concerned we all know that in spring the earth brings forth her abundance of new birth and growth. In summer, the sun shines the hottest and fires rage angrily through tinder-dry vegetation. In autumn, there are mists, vapours and 'mellow fruitfulness'. In winter, the earth is bare so as better to reveal the firmament.

The sun is the greatest entity in the physical world, and provides the earth with light, life and warmth, 'When we consider his functions we must believe that the sun is the soul, or, more intelligibly, the mind of the universe, the ruling principle and divinity of Nature. The sun provides the world with light and takes away darkness: he blacks out and lights up the rest of the stars. The sun controls the change of the seasons and the continual regeneration of the year, following nature's practice. He dispels the gloomy aspect of heaven and lightens the clouds over men's minds.' (Pliny, *Natural History*).

The moon comes next after the sun as the earth's ruling principle, since she controls the tides, liquids as well as mankind's moods and emotions, 'Indeed Phoebe [the moon] is to such an extent a source and influence on all liquids, that according to her waxing and waning she directs and controls not only the waves of the sea, but also the bone-marrow and brains in all living things as well as the sap of trees and plants. When she is deprived of her full light you will notice that all things lose their fullness. But when she has attained her complete roundness, you will find that bones are full of marrow, heads of brains, and other things of sap.' (Giraldus Cambrensis)

Planet earth, the home of mankind, the birth-place and the last resting-place of all humanity, this small speck of dust in an ocean of infinity, over which men kill and maim each other in order to possess only a fraction of its surface. We loot and destroy our own home, planet earth, not out of necessity but merely to fulfil and satisfy our greedy, wanton and extravagant desires. As Thoreau put it, 'What is the use of a house if you haven't got a tolerable planet to put it on?'

We moderns seemed to have learnt very little of true value and wisdom over the last two thousand years, since Pliny stated, 'Earth...the one part of the world of nature on which we have bestowed the title of 'mother' out of the highest respect because she deserves this. Earth is the province of men, as the sky is the province of God. Earth receives us when we are born and feeds us after birth and always supports us, and, at the very end embraces us in her bosom, sheltering us like a mother... She is the only element which is never angry with man. Water turns to rain, and freezes as hail, swells up in waves, and falls headlong in torrents. The air grows thick with clouds and unleashes its fury in storms. Earth, however, is kind, gentle, indulgent, always a servant to man's needs, productive when compelled to be, or lavish of her own accord...For what delights and affronts does she not afford mankind? She is dumped into the sea, or excavated to provide channels. She is tortured at all hours by water, iron, wood, fire, stone and crops, and by far more besides to serve our pleasures rather than our needs.

'Yet so that what she suffers on her surface, her outermost skin, may seem bearable by comparison, we penetrate her inmost parts, digging into her veins of gold and silver and deposits of copper and lead. We search for gems and certain very small stones by sinking shafts into the depths. We drag out earth's entrails; we seek a jewel to wear on a finger... Yet this is the work of a kind goddess, because all these outlets, from which wealth is derived, lead to crime, bloodshed and wars. We sprinkle our blood on Earth and cover her with our unburied bones. Yet when our madness has, as it were, been purified, she herself covers these bones and hides the crimes of mortals...

'...this dot in the universe, as the majority of savants have taught – for this is all the earth is in the context of the whole universe – and this then is the substance of our glory, this is its home, here we fill positions of power and here we covet wealth and put mankind into a turmoil repeatedly and fight wars – even civil wars – and empty the land by killing one another.

'To sum up the outward madness of nations, this is the land in which we drive out our neighbours and dig up and steal their turf to add to our own, so that he who has marked his acres most widely and driven off his neighbours may rejoice in possessing an infinitesimal part of the earth.' (Pliny the Elder, *Natural History*)

Just as in Pliny's times the earth and its wild inhabitants are being attacked on all fronts, and probably at an ever increasing rate and intensity than two thousand years ago, since techno-industrial 'civilisation' has now conquered the entire globe. The earth and its natural bounty are being looted, damaged, destroyed and consumed, through our own neglect, ignorance, cynicism, greed and selfishness. Yet how shall we inhabit a better world if we lose our scenic treasures and natural masterpieces? A better world, possibly, for those whose interests and concerns are purely materialistic, or for those obsessed with speed and efficiency, or for the greedy, the selfish and the cynical, but infinitely worse and depleted and dreary for those whom the great and wondrous 'tree of life' intrigues and delights.

'Various as beauteous, Nature, is thy face;
...all that grows has grace;
All are appropriate – bog, and marsh, and fen,
Are only poor to undiscerning men.' (George Crabbe)

Chapter Thirty-Two

Our 'Pretty Little Love of Nature'

For some sensitive, creative and poetic souls nature, art, literature, history, poetry, dance, artistic creativity and the imagination are far more satisfying than the accumulation of short-lived material possessions, power, prestige, status, or reducing the wonder of life to a mere business enterprise or dull scientific theory. The more practically or pragmatically minded will retort that those sensitive, creative and poetic souls are merely dreamers and idealists, and they probably are, yet...

'I hang 'mid men my needless head,
And my fruit is dreams as theirs is bread,
The goodly men, and the sun-hazed sleeper,
Time shall reap, but after the reaper,
The world shall glean of me, me the sleeper.' (Francis Thomson)

To view politics and economics as the ruling principle of humankind's existence on this earth is a dead-end road, since both view the earth merely as a 'unit of production', and a 'utility' to be 'consumed'. Our present day socio-economic systems lead inevitably to the wasteful consumption of natural resources, as well as the standardisation of the human spirit in an urban sprawl or in an intensively farmed landscape. Materialistic, urbanised, technologically fixated, 'factory' farmed, and industrialised systems have not only brought us the wonders and miracles of science and 'progress', but also pollution, noise, stress, wasteful consumption of finite natural resources, wildlife extinction on an unparalleled scale, and the slow but steady erosion of mankind's cultural diversity (the loss of regional and national costumes, languages, dialects, artistic expressions, craftsmanship, etc). What is the use of all our technological and scientific mastery if we are forced to inhabit a polluted and lifeless world?

How ironic, and indeed karmic, that the very emblem and symbol of the United States of America, the bald eagle, which is meant to represent the best qualities of the American system, that is, liberty, self-reliance, nobility of spirit, was almost wiped out of existence by the very system it represented, as a result of that system's pollutants and the destruction of natural habitats for commercial self-gain. And in a similar vein, the beautiful golden bear, which had been adopted as the symbol and emblem of the Californian state, and was one of the largest and most beautiful species of bear that have ever existed on this planet, became totally extinct by the turn of the twentieth century, following a campaign of extermination officially sanctioned by that Californian state. Today, the quetzal, one of the most beautiful birds of the Americas, the official emblem of Guatemala and a symbol of liberty to the Mayan Indians, is rapidly disappearing as its jungle habitat is logged for timber and cleared for agriculture. If we cannot preserve even the very symbols and emblems which represent liberty and inspiration to our nation-states, then what hope is there for the future of those nation-states?

Our modern day 'love' of nature, as opposed to the Ancient World's spiritual and aesthetic awareness of the living universe, is mere sentimentality and romanticism, since there is nothing particularly lovable about nature. In fact, nature is, if not anti-human, at the least indifferent to humankind. The sun scorches our bare skins, biting insects torment us, we are drenched by lashing rainstorms, the wind chaps our exposed lips, and poisonous creatures and thorny plants, however beautiful to look at, surround our steps. There is something greater to be experienced in the wilds than our sentimental and romantic 'pretty little love of nature' (in the words of D.H. Lawrence), and that is the sense of freedom and spiritual expansion one is able to feel most completely in wild and remote places, as far away as possible from humankind, and his devious and manipulative systems. Only among wild nature is it possible to most fully experience the beauty, mystery and wonder of life, and to have a corresponding awareness of the pettiness, futility and brevity of all our human endeavours and struggles.

All of humankind's scientific miracles, technologies, politics and philosophies are no more than pretty bubbles in the air in the face of Nature's infinity and eternity. The author and zoologist Ivan T. Sanderson experienced similar emotions in the vast tropical rain-forests of West Africa which he visited in the 1930s: 'To dwell amidst this endless foliage is akin to life amongst the gods of old. Past, present, and future have no meaning; the eternity of nature becomes something real. To sit alone in the midday silence of the jungle and try to visualize the machinations of civilized life is an impossibility. All the arts and histories of men become so futile and ephemeral before the grandiose stature of eternal nature, that it seems somehow unaccountable and altogether crazy to imagine little humans believing that their comic and futile efforts count for anything at all. The whole human race becomes just a phase of natural history that will pass like the great dinosaurs of old, leaving not a trace of their worries and their cares. How strongly one feels that, when this and many other self-important herds of striving beings are gone, the forests will remain basking in the sunlight, lords of the earth, unconquerable, perhaps divine.'

It is the modern-day mechanistic and materialistic view of life which is primarily responsible for the wasteful consumption of the earth and its life forms, since if we believe the earth is merely a dead globe of rock and metal, then we must also view all animals, being of nature and of the earth, as mechanistic and soulless as well. This entirely cynical view that animals are soulless automatons who display just automatic and instinctual responses to stimuli (apart of course from humankind and perhaps some primates, and it was not so very long ago when the white man believed other human races were like the 'inferior' animals) flies in the face of common sense, and the direct experience of anyone who has worked or lived with animals (such as field naturalists as opposed to 'closet' and laboratory scientists). Charles Darwin realized this a century and a half ago when he said, 'Animals are our fellow brethren, in suffering, disease and death.' (Darwin, *The Origin of Species*)

Human beings are different to animals only in the degree to which they possess the faculties or powers of reason, self-consciousness, intelligence, learning, memory, instinct, etc. The field naturalist Ernest Thompson Seton, who spent a lifetime studying animals in the wild and not merely in a laboratory, says in his book *Wild Animals I Have Known*, 'We and the beasts are kin. Man has nothing that the animals have not at least a vestige of, the animals have nothing that man does not in some degrees share. Since, then, the animals are creatures with wants and feelings differing in degree only from our own, they surely have their rights. This fact, now beginning to be recognized by the Caucasian world, was first proclaimed by Moses [Exodus 20:10,

Exodus 23:4, Exodus 23:5 and Exodus 23:12] and was emphasized by the Buddhist over two thousand years ago.' Concerning the cruel trapping of wild animals for their fur, for their hides or for 'pest control', Ernest Thompson Seton has this to say, 'Have the wild things no moral or legal rights? What right has man to inflict such long and fearful agony on a fellow-creature, simply because that creature does not speak his language?' Voltaire in his *Philosophical Dictionary* showed that the concept of animals as unthinking and unfeeling machines (as in Descartes' doctrine) ran counter to the empirical evidence.

Humankind's self-proclaimed superiority over the animals, due to our supposed powers of reason, self-consciousness, manipulation, learning and intelligence, does not necessarily make us at all times and in all places a kinder, wiser or nobler species. It is not always nature, but often humankind, who is 'red in tooth and claw', cruel and wasteful, since nature is neither fundamentally cruel nor fundamentally kind, since she is without mankind's moral compass: 'Man, the arch-destroyer and predator in all Creation, whose history is degraded and disgraced in every generation by its record of ruthless destruction and brutality inflicted in greed or lust on the animal creation and on his fellow-man alike, is wont to describe the law of nature in such hackneyed and unthinking phrases as 'red in tooth and claw', and yet may search the operation of that law in vain for similar perpetration of cruelty by wild creatures.' (Gavin Maxwell, *The House of Elrig*)

It is in humankind's own best interests, let alone the preservation of the natural world for its own sake, to wisely manage and thoughtfully conserve the wildlife and the natural resources of this planet, and not to consume or to pollute, whether through greed, ignorance, carelessness, callousness, or sheer wantonness, the very life-blood upon which all life-forms depend for survival: the earth, the airs, the waters, the woods and the metals.

Pythagoras wisely pointed out the folly and short-sightedness of humankind's cruelty to animals over two thousand years ago: 'For as long as man continues to be the ruthless destroyer of lower living beings, he will never know health or peace. For as long as men massacre animals, they will kill each other. Indeed, he who sows the seeds of murder and pain cannot reap joy and love.'

Chapter Thirty-Three

Human Needs and Human Greeds

The spread of scientific 'progress', modern technologies, and so-called 'civilisation' (which derives from the Latin word 'civitas' meaning 'city'), over the entire planet over the past five hundred years (mainly by the imperial European powers), has not necessarily brought its supposed health, wealth and happiness to all of humankind. In fact, many millions of people in the so-called 'Third World' (those ex-colonies of the European powers) are now subsisting at a lower standard of living than they were before they were colonised and 'civilised'. This 'civilisation' was imposed on native peoples to (purportedly) bring them the superior technological and scientific benefits of Western civilisation, yet also to provide a cheap labour force and a huge market for Western goods. Other native peoples were outrightly enslaved, exterminated, and forced into economic servitude by the Western powers.

Apart from the destruction of ancient cultures, slavery, servitude, exploitation, the lowering of living standards and the breaking up of primitive communal societies, Westernisation also brought in its wake many other disadvantages, which were never experienced by the natives or 'savages' before they were 'civilised', such as overcrowding in slums and cities; chemical, industrial and environmental pollution; huge and unprecedented loss of game and natural habitats; warfare on a scale never before experienced with more destructive and pernicious weapons, such as land mines and chemical bombs; the spread of infectious diseases once confined to localised regions; and the steady loss of tribal languages, local dialects, national and folk costumes in a mass, globalised, homogenised culture, a world culture of purely functional uniformity.

Is humankind really progressing or advancing to a higher, wiser, healthier, wealthier, happier existence, or are we just advancing in the medical, technological, material and scientific fields of human endeavour (and even then only readily available for the wealthy few)? In any case, all this 'progress' seems to be at the expense of our natural environment, the beauty and diversity of nature, as well as at the expense of our own human cultural diversity, 'O civilisation, with your million conventions...vain education for the little ones...unnatural craving for cleanliness, feverish striving after comforts that bring no comfort to the heart, are you a mistake altogether?...Ah yes, we are all vainly seeking after happiness in the wrong way. We had only to conquer nature, find out her secrets, make her our obedient slave, then the world would be Eden, and every man Adam and every woman Eve. We are still bravely marching on, conquering Nature, but how weary and sad we are getting! The old joy in life and gaiety of heart have vanished, though we do sometimes pause for a few moments in our long forced march to watch the labours of some pale mechanician seeking after perpetual motion, and indulge in a little, dry, cackling laugh at his expense.' (W.H. Hudson)

Nature can provide indefinitely for human needs but not for human greeds, Gandhi once said[4], but this wise maxim of Gandhi has been conveniently ignored by modern 'civilisation' in order to pursue its selfish, short-term desires and wants. It is only right and fair that everybody should deserve higher living standards, better health, improved hygiene, higher education, more efficient transport, and so on, but 'progress' must be sustainable, or we damn our fellow man and all future generations to a polluted, degraded, wasted environment.

Science, technology, 'progress' and 'civilisation' have provided humankind with amazing comforts and luxuries, rapid transport and communications, improved health and hygiene, great art, profound knowledge, and spectacular entertainments, but what is the use of all these benefits if they bring no comfort to the heart and to the soul, or do not provide humankind with simple, uncomplicated pleasures? The greatest health, wealth and happiness does not necessarily proceed from the accumulation of material luxuries and goods (since it is possible to lead a healthy and frugally comfortable existence in simple surroundings as it is in extravagant ones, if one is wise and prudent), or from the feverish scrabble for prestige and esteem from one's peers, or from power, or from fame, or from a massive fortune, or even from

---

[4] Gandhi also said perspicaciously, 'If it took England the exploitation of half the globe to be what it is today, how many globes will it take India?'

fine works of art, for art has always been a matter of taste and preference, but rather from the beauty, wonder, mystery, and inspiration of nature and life itself.

'The power, beauty and grace of the wild creature, its perfect harmony in nature, the exquisite correspondence between organism, form and faculties, and the environment, with the plasticity and intelligence for the readjustment of the vital machinery, daily, hourly, momentarily, to meet all changes in the conditions, all contingencies; and thus, amidst perpetual permutations and conflict with hostile and destructive forces, to perpetuate a form, a type, a species for thousands and millions of years! – all this was always present to my mind; yet even so it was but a lesser element in the complete feeling. The main thing was the wonderfulness and eternal mystery of life itself; this formative, informing energy – this flame that burns in and shines through the case, the habit, which in lighting another dies, and albeit dying yet endures forever; and the sense, too, that this flame of life was one, and of my kinship with it in all its appearances, in all organic shapes, however different from the human. Nay, the very fact that the forms were unhuman but served to heighten the interest: the roe-deer, the leopard and wild horse, the swallow cleaving the air, the butterfly toying with a flower, and the dragonfly dreaming on the river; the monster whale, the silver flying-fish, and the nautilus with rose and purple tinted sails spread to the wind.' (W.H. Hudson, *The Book of a Naturalist*)

Lord Byron also expressed the mystery and wonder of nature, and its correspondence with mankind, in the following lines:

'There is a pleasure in the pathless woods,
There is a rapture on the lonely shore,
There is society where none intrudes
By the deep sea, and music in its roar:
I love not man the less but nature more,
From these interviews, in which I steal
From all I may be, or have been before,
To mingle with the universe, and feel
What I can ne'er express, yet cannot well conceal.'

Chapter Thirty-Four

Health, Wealth and Happiness

Is humankind progressing or advancing down the centuries into a higher, wiser, nobler, better state of being, or is that concept just a fallacy, a myth, a fiction, a poorly-judged utopian dream, and an ideal invented by the philistines of material progress to justify the wastefulness and selfishness of their system, or to partially salve their consciences? Medicine and surgical practices have undoubtedly advanced and become highly developed, even miraculous, but has medicine advanced only in order to keep up with the spread of infectious diseases around the world, once confined to remote or localised regions, as well as to keep up with the spread of 'dis-ease' and stress due to modern lifestyles (and thus heart disease and cancers) and to greater environmental pollution? In any case, can science and technology, however miraculous and awe-inspiring, make humankind more compassionate, more humane, more kind, more caring, more tolerant, more selfless, more honest, more brave, more reverent, and more prudent, or merely supply humankind's demands for a more comfortable and profligate lifestyle?

Has there really been a slow but steady 'march of progress' down the centuries, from primitive 'savagery' to 'semi-barbarism' to enlightened modern Western 'civilisation'? 'Civilisation' has indeed provided humankind with comforts and luxuries, rapid communications, fantastic entertainments, etc, but have all these 'miracles' of science and technology provided a greater degree of general happiness and contentment? According to the author Herman Melville who lived among the Polynesian 'savages' of the Marquesas Islands in the nineteenth century, civilised life does not lead to a greater degree of happiness and health:

'As I extended my wanderings in the valley and grew more familiar with the habits of its inmates, I was fain to confess that, despite the disadvantages of his condition, the Polynesian savage, surrounded by all the luxurious provisions of nature, enjoyed an infinitely happier, though a certainly less intellectual existence, than the self-complacent European.

'The naked wretch who shivers beneath the bleak skies, and starves among the inhospitable wilds of Tierra del Fuego, might indeed be made happier by civilisation, for it would alleviate his physical wants. But the voluptuous Indian, with every desire supplied, whom Providence has bountifully provided with all the sources of pure and natural enjoyment, and from whom are removed so many of the ills and pains of life – what has he to desire at the hands of Civilisation? She may 'cultivate his mind', may 'elevate his thoughts' – these I believe are the established phrases – but will he be the happier? Let the once smiling and populous Hawaiian Islands, with their now diseased, starving, and dying natives, answer the question...In a primitive state of society, the enjoyments of life, though few and simple, are spread over a great extent, and are unalloyed; but Civilisation, for every advantage she imparts, holds a hundred evils in reserve – the heart-burnings, the jealousies, the social rivalries, the family dissensions, and the thousand self-inflicted discomforts of refined life, which make up in units the swelling aggregate of human misery, are unknown among these unsophisticated people...

'The fiend-like skill we display in the invention of all manner of death-dealing engines, the vindictiveness with which we carry on our wars, and the misery and desolation that follow in their train, are enough of themselves to distinguish the white civilised man as the most ferocious animal on the face of the earth...

'But it is needless to multiply the examples of civilised barbarity; they far exceed in the amount of misery they cause the crimes which we regard with such abhorrence in our less enlightened fellow-creatures...

'The term 'savage' is, I conceive, often misapplied, and indeed when I consider the vices, cruelties, and enormities of every kind that spring up in the tainted atmosphere of a feverish civilisation, I am inclined to think that so far as the relative wickedness of the parties is concerned, four or five Marquesan Islanders sent to the United States as missionaries might be quite as useful as an equal number of Americans dispatched to the Islands in a similar capacity...

'But the continual happiness, which so far as I was able to judge appeared to prevail in the valley, sprang principally from that all-pervading sensation which Rousseau has told us he at one time experienced, the mere buoyant sense of a healthful physical existence. And indeed in this particular the Typees had ample reason to felicitate themselves, for sickness was almost unknown. During the whole period of my stay I saw but one invalid among them; and on their smooth clear skins you observed no blemish or mark of disease.' (Melville, *Typee*)

In the modern Western world with nature now conquered, controlled and manipulated for our urban civilisation, and the imagination now de-throned in favour of analytical, reductionist, scientific, left-hand brain perception, has the earth really become a better and happier place to inhabit? Humankind needs nature and the wilderness as inspiration for our spiritual and poetic requirements, to reaffirm and to recollect our oneness with all of Creation, as well as for recreation, health, and maintaining the ecological well-being of the entire planet.

'What would the world be, once bereft

Of wet and of wildness? Let them be left,

O let them be left, wildness and wet,

Long live the weeds and the wilderness yet.' (Gerald Manley Hopkins)

The words 'progress' and 'in the interests of economic development' are too readily mouthed by politicians, scientists and economists. But how is it possible to actually measure such a process, if such a process does exist in the first place, and perhaps only in the minds of bureaucrats and profiteers. Scientific progress has of course given the affluent classes many comforts and miracles, yet all this material progress has brought in its wake ecological havoc, cultural homogenisation, and self-seeking philistinism. Have human nature or human morals been improved by science and technology? Or are we more selfish, more unscrupulous, more money-grabbing, more cynical, more corrupt, and more uncaring in Western civilisation? And, in addition, our not so distant ancestors lived in a far cleaner and more culturally diverse planet before industrialisation, city living, imperial conquest and Western colonisation.

Wild nature, with all of its beauty, wonder and harshness, has been controlled, conquered, tamed, domesticated, or farmed over. Modern, urban man is incredibly dull and colourless in comparison with his wild, individualistic, pre-industrialised predecessors with their adventurous, dangerous lifestyles and fantastical clothes: the picturesque 'savage' of North America (as illustrated and painted by George Catlin), the warrior, the adventurer, and the aristocrat-poet (such as Sir Walter Raleigh, Lord Byron or Edward John Trelawney), have been replaced by the 'corporate' business man, who craves security and conformity to bourgeois values. The freedom-loving shepherd, cowboy, gaucho, Native American warrior, Cossack, etc, have long disappeared, or become 'modernised' and 'civilised'. Rapidly disappearing now too are the 'savages' of Amazonia, West Africa, and South-East Asia, as their forest homelands are 'opened up' for 'development', that is, logging and exploitation. And when humankind has become one homogenised, uniform, monotonous whole, but abundant with materialistic comforts and luxuries for the affluent few, and with all of nature, outside of a few nature reserves, controlled, built over or farmed over, will we all really be happier, healthier and wiser?

Even the reckless and criminal societies of men have disappeared into the pages of history as society has become more 'civilised', since the pirate, the Viking, the whaler, the highwayman, the bushranger, the brigand, the Wild West bandit, and the gunslinger no longer exist anywhere on earth. For though they were self-seeking criminals and butchers of often defenceless people and animals, they also often displayed a romantic wildness and a reckless bravery, and when united with mobility and freedom of movement as well, in the form of the noble horse (as in the case of the cowboy, the gaucho, the Cossack, the Native American warrior of the prairies, the highwayman, the bushranger, and the Wild west bandit), or in the form of a beautifully crafted ship (of the pirate, the Viking and the whaler), or simply through the peregrinations of the peaceful, wandering shepherd with his flocks and herds on the hills or in the mountains, then here we have the ultimate freedom only dreamed of by sedentary, office-bound, house-bound, 'civilised' man. The steppes and the Cossacks, the gauchos and the pampas, the cowboys and the ranges, the Native American warriors and the prairies, the highwaymen and the heathlands, the shepherds and the downlands, have been almost all swept away, ploughed up, built over, and farmed over, in order to supply the demands of our urban, industrialised civilisation. Science, technology and 'progress' may have advanced in miraculous ways, but this has been at the expense of wild nature, the 'picturesque' and the diversity of our own human culture.

It seems the beautiful wilds and our cultural diversity are destined to be completely sacrificed on the altar of materialism, in order to allow the already affluent to lead ever more extravagant, wasteful, secure and comfortable lifestyles. And as always in 'civilised' life, short-term greed and commercial self-gain hold sway over humankind's long-term spiritual, aesthetic, artistic and creative needs and requirements.

The great Arab historian Ibn Khaldun realized the perils and the pleasures of civilised life centuries ago when he said, 'The goal of civilisation is settled life and the achievement of luxury. But there is a limit which cannot be overstepped. When prosperity and luxury come to a people they are followed by excessive consumption and extravagance...[whereby] the human soul itself is undermined, both in its worldly well-being and in its spiritual life.' (Wood, *Legacy: A Search for the Origins of Civilisation*)

Chapter Thirty-Five

As Good As It Gets

Is modern, Western civilisation really 'as good as it gets', have we really 'never had it so good', and are we truly at the 'end of history' (to quote the title of a book by a famous modern historian), or is Western 'liberal democracy' (left wing or right wing or middling) in reality just another phase of humankind's evolution, both good and ill, progressive and recidivist, and particularly obsessed in the present era with scientific and technological achievements.

Science, technology and materialism will not of themselves lead humankind to a Utopia or Eden on earth, since we would already be there by now, but it is just as much leading us all to an artificial, wasteful and selfish society, a society of mass production, mass consumption and mass wastage, with lifeless, sprawling metropolises and third-world shanty towns, and where the citizens of such urban conglomerations attend their offices, laboratories, factories, warehouses, schools and churches in order to worship '...a little god of their own little imaginations, who did not create and does not regard the swallow and dove and white egret and bird of paradise, and who therefore was not my god and whose will as they understood it was nothing to me.' (W.H. Hudson) If a religion or a system or a society does not serve to make humankind more humane to his fellow creatures, both human and animal, then it does not matter at all if all those religions and systems are wiped off the face of the earth, or we were all, each and every one of us 'sun-worshippers, like the Persians, as well as Christians; also that we were Buddhists, and worshippers of our dead ancestors like the Chinese, and that we were pagans and idolators who bow down to sticks and stones if all these added cults would serve to make us more reverent.' (W. H. Hudson)

Though in the Western world the most glaring examples of cruelty to the animal creation have been generally outlawed everywhere (such as bear baiting, cock fighting, dog fighting, otter hunting, badger baiting, etc) other wanton cruelties perpetrated by humans against animals continue unabated, such as hare coursing, wildfowling, deer hunting, etc. The hunters would retort that accusations of cruelty by gun or dog against certain species of animal are sentimental and mawkish, yet they should remember that '...no form of cruelty inflicted, whether for sport or profit or from some other motive, on the lower animals has ever died out of itself in the land. Its end has invariably been brought about by legislation through the devotion of men who were the 'cranks', the 'faddists', the 'sentimentalists', of their day, who were jeered and laughed at by their fellows, and who only succeeded by sheer tenacity and force of character after long fighting against public opinion and a reluctant parliament, in finally getting their law.' (W.H. Hudson)

Compared to other countries the appalling number of motorised vehicles on the United Kingdom's overcrowded highways and byways is quite astonishing (such as compared to Russia at present), and when one considers how traffic-free our roads would seem to us today if we were to travel back in time eighty or ninety years, then the following statement written in the early twentieth century seems so quaint and astonishingly naïve: 'The stream invites us to follow- the impulse is so common that it might be set down as an instinct; and certainly there is no more fascinating pastime than to keep company with a river from its source to the sea. Unfortunately this is not easy in a country where running waters have been enclosed, which should be as free as the rain and sunshine to all, and were once free, when England was England still, before landowners annexed them, even as they annexed or stole the commons and shut up the footpaths and made it an offence for a man to go aside from the road to feel God's grass under his feet. Well, they have also got the road now, and cover and blind and choke us with its dust and insolently hoot-hoot at us. Out of the way, miserable crawlers, if you don't want to be smashed!! They have got the roads and have a parliament of motorists to maintain them in possession, but it yet remains to be seen whether or not they shall be able to keep them.' (W. H. Hudson)

Even as far back as the middle of the nineteenth century the English author Thomas De Quincey was deploring the destructive and unnecessary building of roads, which even back then was spoiling the peace and beauty of the English countryside (let him rise from his grave today and see how much more of the English countryside has been spoilt by motorways and roads, he would surely be horror-struck!).

'...The cottage and the valley concerned in this description were not imaginary: the valley was the lovely one, in those days, of Grasmere; and the cottage was occupied for more than twenty years by myself...Thirty years ago, a gang of Vandals (nameless, I thank heaven, to me), for the sake of building a mail-coach road that never would be wanted, carried, at a cost of £3000 to the defrauded parish, a horrid causeway of sheer granite masonry, for three-quarters-of-a-mile, right through the loveliest succession of secret forest dells and shy recesses of the lake, margined by unrivalled ferns, amongst which was the Osmunda regalis...' (Thomas De Quincey, *Confessions of an English Opium-Eater*)

If humankind, in its mad desire for self-gain, material goods, speed, efficiency and control, is to wipe off the face of the earth all of our beautiful wild heritage, then what would there be left to inspire man's soul? Man would indeed 'die from a great loneliness of spirit' without the mystical sensation or feeling which only wild nature can supply: the sense that man is but a small part of the universe, a small part of a greater whole, an integral part, along with all of Creation, of this living, wondrous universe, and akin to all other life-forms; and also the feeling of melancholy, mingled with joyfulness, at the brevity of our earthly span, and at the beauty and transience of all living, and indeed inanimate, things. These feelings or sensations of joy, melancholy, mysticism, and a correspondence between man and nature appear to be an eternal part of the soul of man, since they are to be discovered in all great works of nature art, poetry and literature from every land and every era since the literary and fine arts were first created. As far as art, poetry and literature in the English-speaking nations are concerned (as well as some other nationals, such as the Russians, whose literary works have been translated into English, and thus able to be read by the author), the greatest authors and artists of the natural world would have to include the following persons:

(1) William Henry Hudson and his romantic tales set among the wild pampas, jungles and deserts of South America in the middle of the nineteenth century, before those regions were spoiled by 'progress'. Hudson wrote strange, haunting stories about his travels and life there, or semi-fictional tales full of danger, adventure, and eccentric or roguish characters. His best works include *Green Mansions: A Romance of the Tropical Forest*, *The Purple Land That*

England Lost, El Ombu, Nino Diablo, Marta Riquelme, Idle Days in Patagonia, Far Away and Long Ago, and *The Naturalist in La Plata.* Then there are also Hudson's travel books about England describing the English countryside and wildlife (before the destructive practices of modern, scientific farming), as well as the interesting human characters he encountered on his rambles, such as *The Book of a Naturalist, Afoot in England, A Shepherd's Life,* and *A Traveller in Little Things.*

(2) Richard Jefferies and his weird, idiosyncratic and visionary autobiography called *The Story of My Heart,* which describes his mystical and pantheistic view of the natural world.

(3) The very eccentric but brilliant naturalist and pioneering conservationist Charles Waterton, and his colourful travel book *Wanderings in South America.*

(4) Charles Darwin and his incredible voyage by ship around the world in the *Beagle,* and his descriptions of wild and remote lands then relatively unspoilt by 'progress' in his book *The Voyage of the Beagle.*

(5) The brilliant eighteenth-century field naturalist Gilbert White and his classic descriptions of the local wildlife of an English parish in *The Natural History of Selbourne.*

(6) Herman Melville and his haunting, mystical novel *Moby Dick,* which is also a veritable encyclopaedia about the lore and natural history of whales, as well as his adventurous book *Typee* about his life in the Marquesas Islands with the natives there.

(7) Ivan Turgenev and his book *A Hunter's Album* with its vivid descriptions of the wild nature and strange characters of Russia's vast steppe-lands and forests, which were still relatively unspoilt in the middle of the nineteenth century.

(8) The German author, traveller and natural scientist Alexander von Humboldt and his book *Travels in South America* about his amazing journeys around the jungles and mountains of South and Central America in the nineteenth century.

(9) Henry Walter Bates and his journey all the way up the Amazon River in which he collected and categorised all the wildlife he discovered, and which he vividly describes in his book *Naturalist on the Amazon.*

(10) Ernest Thompson Seton and his interesting and empathetic wild animal stories, which are set in the Wild West of America and in the backwoods of Canada, where the author lived, worked and

travelled in the nineteenth century. His best collection of stories is in his book *Wild Animals I Have Known.*

(11) The solitary nature mystic, self-sufficiency guru and visionary Henry David Thoreau and his thought-provoking book *Walden: Life Among the Woods.*

(12) The writer, artist and explorer George Catlin and his sympathetic and un-romanticised account of the customs and lifestyles of the Native American Indians, amongst whom he travelled and lived extensively in the nineteenth century, just prior to their conquest and subsequent demise at the hands of the white American invaders, as described in his book *North American Indians.* His beautiful and invaluable paintings and drawings of Indians in their native costumes are also a source of wonder and inspiration.

(13) John James Audubon and his marvellous natural history paintings as well as his adventurous life in the wilds of North America. It was Audubon's ambition to paint every single species of bird and mammal native to the North Americas (which he almost achieved!).

(14) The eighteenth-century Swedish botanist Carl von Linne (Carolus von Linnaeus) and his ambition to catalogue every known species of plant and animal on earth, and who invented the modern system of classification.

(15) The zoologist Ivan T. Sanderson and his wonderful and descriptive books (*Animal Treasure* and *Caribbean Treasure*) about his animal collecting expeditions in the 1930s to West Africa and to the South and Central Americas.

(16) The brilliant medieval writer Gerald of Wales (Giraldus Cambrensis) and his books about the customs, traditions, natural history, and supernatural tales of Ireland and Wales back in the twelfth century (his tales and stories are real gems of the story-teller's art).

(17) The Roman author and natural scientist Pliny the Elder and his huge, encyclopaedic book *Pliny's Natural History* describing almost everything then known about the natural world.

(18) The English author, explorer, archaeologist, ethnologist and mystic P. H. Fawcett who mysteriously disappeared in the jungles of South America during one of his journeys of exploration there in the 1920s. His travel book *Exploration Fawcett* vividly describes his amazing and dangerous journeys in the then wild and unexplored jungles of South America, and the native wildlife and people he discovered.

(19) The 'peasant poet' John Clare and his beautiful, mystical and vivid nature poetry.

(20) The author, artist and engraver Thomas Bewick who excelled in portraying the quaint, humble, harsh and unspoilt life of the English countryside, both animal and human, in the eighteenth century.

(21) The English author EHA and his humorous descriptions, as well as mystical musings, about the human and wild inhabitants of Western India, in his book *A Naturalist on the Prowl*.

(22) The big-game hunter, author and naturalist F. C. Selous and his book about his expeditions in South-East Africa (*Travel and Adventure in South-East Africa*). This book is quite shocking in its descriptions of the senseless and wasteful slaughter of game animals in Africa in the nineteenth century, but it is also a vivid account of South-East African wildlife, natives and scenery before that part of the world was colonised and developed.

Other great authors who wrote classic natural history books include Jim Corbett (who wrote books about tigers and other wildlife in the Indian jungles of the 1920s and 1930s); Frank Dufesne (who wrote a classic book describing his journeys in the forests of the Pacific north west of America in the 1960s, where he studied grizzly bears); Gerald Durrell and his many humorous and interesting books about his animal collecting expeditions all over the world, as well as his autobiographical trilogy describing his idyllic childhood in Corfu in the 1930s; Fred G. Merfield who wrote about his expeditions in West Africa in the 1930s, where he studied gorillas and the local wildlife and natives; and, finally, the Polish author Arkady Fiedler who wrote an interesting book about an animal collecting expedition he undertook up the Amazon River in the 1940s.

Writers in whose literary works can be discovered a sense of the supernatural or divine in nature and in the landscape, and an un-sentimentalised account of the horror, brutality, and violence of nature and the 'primitive' lifestyle, as well as an acknowledgement of nature's kind or tender side, include among the very best in that field the Ukrainian-Jewish author Isaac Babel, the Russian-Ukrainian author Nikolai Gogol, the Anglo-Argentine author W.H. Hudson and the Anglo-Irish author W.B.Yeats.

All of these authors came into contact with, or lived amongst, primitive and 'savage' peoples (the Gaelic Irish peasantry, the Argentine gauchos, and the Ukrainian Cossacks), and tried hard to understand the mentality of 'primitive', pre-industrial, 'uncivilised' man. Yet in spite of the oftentimes harshness and brutality of the 'primitive' life, away from the city and 'civilisation', they all believed that the 'savage' or the peasant or the herdsman lived a more fulfilled, freer and more richly imaginative and individualistic existence than their 'civilised' counterparts. They also realised that 'civilised' man can never really return or go back to a more natural, primitive existence since he is now 'out of her [Nature], having made our own conditions; and our conditions have reacted upon us and made us what we are – artificial creatures. Nature is now something pretty to go and look at occasionally, but not too often, nor for too long a time…' (W. H. Hudson).

In the stories of Gogol the world is a surreal, spacey and highly amusing place: is the moon jiggling about in the vision of a drunken Cossack, or is the devil actually playing ball with it? People suddenly resemble inanimate objects such as a tea-pot, and everything is alive and resonant with a meaning beyond just its mere physical appearance.

In the stories of Isaac Babel the Russian landscape is violently coloured with blood-red sunsets and cruel, marauding Cossacks, who commit the most appalling crimes yet have their own sense of morality and brotherhood, and you get a vivid sense of the brutality, anarchy and senseless, random violence of the Russian Civil War.

The violent yet freedom-loving world of the Argentine gaucho, and a country teeming with unspoilt nature and curious or colourful wildlife, live forever in the South American romances and tales of William Henry Hudson.

The short stories of W. B. Yeats wonderfully bring back to life the brooding spirituality, superstitions and everyday magical beliefs of the Gaelic Irish peasantry, both in his own era and in ancient pagan Ireland.

Chapter Thirty-Six

A Little Space

Can modern civilisation not even leave a little space in this busy, technologically-fixated world for wild nature and the unspoilt wilderness? In a world of Big Business, the play of market forces, economic necessity, commercialism, self-gain, consumerism, speed, efficiency, and utilitarianism, where can the beautiful and un-sanitised world of nature find a space to inhabit? Since in such a society the environment must be 'socially hygienic', sanitised, sterilised, smooth, respectable, trim, tidy, and chemically clean, like an all-encompassing municipal town park, and in that highly managed garden we should all be homogenised, image-conscious, domesticated, dutiful and dull, in other words, petit bourgeois. Is the sole purpose of our existence on this earth really so base as to just amount to 'getting a job' and scrabbling after wealth, personal possessions and power? Concern for the natural world should not necessarily have to be in any way 'useful' to science or commerce or medicine or academic knowledge, or any other utilitarian or material purpose one might think fit. Some souls on this earth may wish to dissect nature for whatever base or noble purposes they think it might serve, but for other souls the beauty, wonder and mystery of nature in and of itself is the true wellspring and ultimate inspiration for humankind's spiritual and poetic yearnings:

'Here I lay and communed...There were no signs of men, no sounds of human life... nothing but a sighing wind and a sort of earth-murmur under the trees, and I used to think that God, whatever He was, or the great spiritual forces that I believed lay behind all phenomena... must be nearer to one's consciousness in places like this than among the bustling of men in the towns and houses. As the material world faded away among the shadows, I felt dimly the real spiritual world behind shining through...I meditated on the meaning of these dreams till the veil over outer things seemed very thin; diving down into my inner consciousness as deeply as I could till a stream of tremendous yearning for the realities that lay behind appearances poured out of me in to the night.' (Algernon Blackwood)

Nature, the imagination, art, poetry, music, literature, dance, visions – are these things not preferable to the dull realities and dreary 'business of life'. How dull, mundane, monotonous and commonplace the world becomes when we limit our vision, since humankind needs to escape, at least occasionally, from the confines of its culture and community, and lift its soul 'above this little Earth, this folly-fetter'd world'. (Thomas Warton)

There are some people who would argue that human society is 'progressing' or advancing down the centuries into a higher, wiser and more perfect condition, and that modern Western man has 'never had it so good', with all of our technologies, sciences, domestic appliances and other gadgetry. But, one might validly ask, what is this society good for, and moreover, for whom? Is the modern Western world better at artistic creativity than the Ancient World or 'primitive' cultures, and has it created a more beautiful environment for us to inhabit? And is the modern, technocratic Western system only beneficial for the privileged elite, but not for the less fortunate members of its society? Anyway, beauty, art and creativity are eternal and last forever in the soul of humankind, as Keats pointed out in his 'Ode to a Grecian Urn'. Art, beauty and creativity do not become more advanced, but merely change and mutate, and yet they last forever.

> 'Then gin I thinke on that which Nature sayd,
> Of that same time when no more change shall be
> But steadfast rest of all things firmely stayed
> Upon the pillours of Eternity.'

Can science, technology and progress on the material sphere make humankind freer, more compassionate, more imaginative, and more humane, or merely allow its everyday material existence to become more comfortable, more extravagant, cleaner, faster and more efficient? And do these things really lead to happiness and 'soul-growth', or do they inevitably lead to degeneracy since 'the ending of passion and strife is the beginning of decay' (in the words of W.H. Hudson). Modern society has given life to a 'Frankenstein's monster' called Science and Technology and which, although in itself not necessarily evil or destructive or negative, has become not a slave to man's needs but a servant to man's 'greeds', and will consume the entire earth on his behalf, in order for humankind (or perhaps only for the privileged elites) to lead ever more decadent and convenient lifestyles.

Is there a dichotomy between the human heart and the human mind, between thought and feeling, between the imagination and reason, between conventional morality and personal conscience, between art and science, between the sacred and the secular, between a mystical concept of nature and a more objective, scientific or dispassionate view of the natural world, between intuition and calculation, between the needs of the individual and the needs of the greater collective society, between the holistic and the analytic, between the passionate, irrational Dionysian abandonment to the will and the measured, controlled Apollonian direction of the will? These are questions which artists have struggled to answer down the centuries, and how humankind is able or unable to reconcile these conflicting interests.

In the present age the 'left hand brainers' (who emphasise reason, logic, and the material world) have gained the upper hand, as they inevitably will in a purely materialistic, technocratic, consumer society, which now generally exists in the Western world. Yet two centuries ago at the beginning of the modern Western system, and the inevitable rise of industrialisation, urban growth, standardisation, and the erosion of rural communities, the Romantic writers, poets and artists had a final, collective artistic and spiritual rebellion against the philistines of material progress. This rebellion more than ever before needs to be rekindled, before we all become slaves to reason, reductionism, empiricism, and materialism (as pointed out by such Romantic writers, artists or poets as Percy Bysshe Shelley, Lord Byron, Samuel Taylor Coleridge, William Blake, William Wordsworth, Thomas De Quincey, Edgar Allen Poe, E.T.A. Hoffmann, Theophile Gautier, Honore Balzac, Nikolai Gogol, Johann Wolfgang von Goethe, Francisco de Goya, Washington Irving, Henry Fuseli, etc).

Is humankind really advancing (spiritually, intellectually, physically, morally, socially) down (or up?) the centuries, that is, a kind of ascent upwards in a linear direction through time from a lower, more 'barbaric' state to a higher, more 'civilised' one: from ape-men to the stone age to the bronze age to the iron age to, eventually, our modern, technocratic, democratic Western system, or, not so long ago for much of the world's population, to a 'Dictatorship of the Proletariat'[5]? Or, on the other hand, is humankind degenerating or regressing down the centuries, and have we 'fallen' or lapsed from a higher, better, more truthful and more beautiful condition in the dim and distant past. That is, as described in the Ancient Greek histories of Hesiod, who believed that mankind once lived in a Golden Age which has since become steadily more and more degraded: from gold to silver to copper to bronze and, finally, to iron, the worst and most pernicious age of all, and the present one. This is similar to the Hindu belief that we are presently living in the Age of Kali, which is the hardest and most evil epoch of all, but eventually Brahma will destroy the Universe and Creation will begin again: new, pure, fresh and innocent. Jewish Talmudic scholars also believe that the intellectual and spiritual quality or calibre of humanity has declined as the generations have proceeded. Or, finally, is there merely a 'sublime recapitulation' of knowledge, good and evil in each generation throughout history. This was believed by the Roman Catholic Church at one time, since everything was set down by God in the beginning, and then the Prophets of Jehovah (in the Old Testament) and finally the Word of Christ (in the New Testament) completed the picture for this earthly span.

These are impossible questions to answer, but war, greed, intolerance, murder, cruelty, bigotry, hatred, corruption, famines, tyranny, and so on, have existed in human societies since the beginnings of recorded time, in whatever era or society, whether stone age, bronze age, iron age, Communist or Capitalist, and they still exist in the present nuclear, steel and machine age. But undoubtedly a large proportion of the world's population in the modern, Western world is able to lead longer, healthier, more comfortable, more convenient, more materialistic and more extravagant lifestyles today than ever before, as a direct result of the application of science, technology, and modern medicine. But all of this 'progress' has been achieved at the expense of the diversity, the beauty and the wildness of the natural world, as well as the ironing out of human diversity, a decline in the craftsmanship of our built environment and of our manufactured

---

[5] Since Marx and Engels believed that human society evolved or progressed from primitive communism to slavery to feudalism to capitalism to socialism and, finally, to true communism.

goods, and the destruction of more communal, tribal, primitive or agricultural/peasant societies, and the age-old traditions, wisdoms and crafts of these folk cultures.

On the one hand we should bless this technocratic, scientific, materialistic, urban civilisation for the comforts, luxuries, domestic appliances, gadgets, rapid communications and transportation it affords us. Yet, on the other hand, we should curse it for the destruction it has wrought against the beautiful, wild world of nature, which has been sacrificed for farmland, quarries and dams, and to provide the necessaries for the huge urban populations which must be supported. We should also curse it for the disappearance of so much age-old wisdom, which was sacrificed when tribal and folk cultures were broken up in the migration to city or town, and when people lost their connection to the earth, the land, the animals, the plants and their fellow man, in pursuit of selfish materialism. Yet it would be foolish now to want to return to the old, rural, tribal, communal, pastoral, or peasant ways, since why would we want to go back to the 'harshnesses' and 'unpredictablenesses' of nature. But this urban civilisation with its lack of poetry for the soul, its rank consumerism, its materialism, its worship of technology, and its conformity to bourgeois values, chafes the free spirit in man day and night (or at least those who have not lost their free spirits to profligacy and materialism).

> 'Let not young souls be smothered out before
> They do quaint deeds and fully flaunt their pride.
> It is the world's one crime its babes grow dull,
> Its poor are ox-like, limp and leaden-eyed.
>
> Not that they starve, but starve so dreamlessly,
> Not that they sow, but that they seldom reap,
> Not that they serve, but have no gods to serve,
> Not that they die, but that they die like sheep.'

(Vachel Lindsay, *The Leaden-Eyed*).

For all of our much-vaunted science and technology are we Westerners really as advanced and as enormously clever as we like to see ourselves, and have the benefits of technological discoveries really improved the human lot? The food we eat, the basic and fundamental necessity of life, is contaminated with agricultural chemicals and, although aesthetically pleasing to the eye on the supermarket shelves, these intensively produced fruits and vegetables of a great size and a perfect, uniform shape have become steadily more and more tasteless to eat and bland on the palate (and that is not even considering the harm to health agricultural chemicals are causing to ourselves, to future generations, as well as to the environment). And this also reveals that modern, capitalist Western society has not been designed for human welfare, but actually for the market-driven, profit-making organisations and institutions which control our lives. That is not to say that technological or scientific progress is of itself an evil or a negative force for humankind, but these forces of progress have been hijacked by self-serving businessmen, scientists and politicians in boardrooms, laboratories and parliaments, for their own material gain and political power.

It seems as if we have merely exchanged the tyranny of the Church and the Landed Aristocracy for the tyranny of the State and Big Business over the past two centuries, in our modern, soulless, overcrowded, dreary, concrete, steel and glass cities. Even our supposedly altruistic, free, State-run schools (which now exist in almost all Western nations) are really just '…factories, with a machinery to unmake and remake, or fabricate, the souls of children.' (W.H. Hudson)

How lamentable it is that of all the wonderful, inventive, creative, communal, or earth-centred societies and cultures that have existed on this earth (but that is not to say that there have ever been any perfect or utopian societies anywhere on this earth), the busy, beastly, Western system has come to dominate the lot, a system not really based on artistic/creative excellence or on quality of life, but on base profitability and economic competition, and is not the Western system the most savage on Earth?

'Cerulean eyes, locks comparable in hue to the "yellow hair that floats on the eastern clouds", and a white body, like snow with a blush on it – what could Nature have been dreaming of when she gave such things to her rudest, most savage humans! That they should have overcome dark-eyed races, and trod on their necks and ruined their works, strikes one as unnatural, and reads like a fable.' (W.H. Hudson)

The market-driven, materialistic, exploitative, mechanistic, business-like, drab, wasteful Western system is dominating the world today, not because that system is necessarily the most excellent and the most advanced system, but it could just as easily be because that system is the most savage and the most barbaric, and because that system has spent the past five hundred years conquering, colonising, destroying, and perverting with the idea of self-gain far older, much wiser, more communal, and more earth-centred cultures. It has destroyed them so completely that in their despair and humiliation they have committed a form of cultural suicide. In their need to survive, these other non-Western cultures have been forced to adopt the more competitive, less communal, and more aggressive cultures of their Western conquerors and taskmasters, who no longer occupy their lands physically but now through world economics. Even the self-centred, once xenophobic Chinese have cast away their traditional, beautiful, colourful, graceful, flowing robes and cut off their Manchu-style pigtails in favour of the comparatively drab, sartorially repressed Western business uniform of shirt, tie, jacket, trousers and short, cropped hair. In the 1920s Liang Shu-Ming warned the Chinese people about the consequences of adopting the Western system, 'The fundamental spirit of China was to seek harmony and synthesis, that of the west to go forward to change: a path which has been destructive of nature, and of the spirit.' (Wood, *Legacy: A Search for the Origins of Civilisation*) Early reports by the Chinese of the first Westerners they encountered (the Spanish in the Philippines) were not complimentary, 'These barbarians have a grim look, untidy hair, an unpleasant smell. They have no rituals worthy of the name. They are liars and are rather arrogant. They conquer countries by fraud and force, ingratiating themselves in a friendly way before they oppress the natives. At the heart of their conduct is violence.' (Wood, *Legacy: A Search for the Origins of Civilisation*)

No race, political or economic system has a monopoly on genius and creativity. Our present day rationalist, reductionist, competitive, complex, technologically sophisticated system will not of itself make humankind a kinder, wiser, more compassionate, more humane, more generous, more just, more caring, more tolerant, more honest, more peaceable, more creative, or more aesthetically intelligent creature, since these are universal qualities of the human soul, but could just as easily make humankind more selfish, more greedy, more shallow, more superficial, more materialistic, more exploitative, more undignified, more vulgar, more smug, more unscrupulous, more cynical, more rapacious, and less concerned with the common good.

Indubitably Western civilisation has turned us into more intellectual beings via the advances of scientific knowledge, technological progress and mass communications, and it has also improved our lot on the material level, yet our primitive yearnings still require communal feelings both for our fellow humans and the fellow creatures we share this planet with, as well as for wild, untamed areas, which provide us with much needed spiritual solace.

'Solitude in the presence of natural beauty and grandeur is the cradle of thoughts and aspirations which are not only good for the individual, but which society could ill do without... Nor is there much satisfaction in contemplating the world with nothing left to the spontaneous activity of nature; with every foot of land brought into cultivation, which is capable of growing food for human beings; every flowery waste or wild pasture ploughed up, all quadrupeds or birds which are not domesticated for man's use exterminated as his rivals for food, every hedgerow or superfluous tree rooted out, and scarcely a place left where a wild shrub or flower could grow without being eradicated as a weed in the name of improved agriculture.'

(John Stuart Mill)

'My aspens dear, whose airy cages quelled,
Quelled or quenched in leaves the leaping sun,
All felled, felled, are all felled;
Of a fresh and following folded rank
Not spared, not one
That dandled a sandalled
Shadow that swam or sank
On meadow and river and wild-wandering weed-winding
bank.

O if we but knew what we do
When we delve or hew –
Hack and rack the growing green!
Since country is so tender
To touch, her being so slender,
That, like this sleek and seeing ball
But a prick will make no eye at all,
Where we, even when we mean
  To mend her we end her;
  when we hew or delve:

After-comers cannot guess the beauty been.
Ten or twelve, only ten or twelve
Strokes of havoc unselve
The sweet especial scene,
Rural scene, a rural scene,
Sweet especial rural scene.'
(Gerard Manley Hopkins, *Binsey Poplars Felled 1879*)

'...By Langley Bush I roam, but the bush hath left its hill,
On Cowper Green I stray, 'tis a desert strange and chill,
And the spreading Lea Close Oak, ere decay had penned its will
To the axe of the Spoiler and self-interest fell a prey,
And Crossberry Way and old Round Oak's narrow lane
With its hollow trees like pulpits I shall never see again,
Enclosure like a Buonaparte let not a thing remain,
It levelled every bush and tree and levelled every hill
And hung the moles for traitors – though the brook is running
 Still
It runs a naked stream, cold and chill...'
(John Clare, *Remembrances*)

'Despite all the land left free
For the first time I feel somehow
That it isn't going to last,
That before I snuff it, the whole
Boiling will be bricked in
Except for the tourist parts...
And that will be England gone,
The shadows, the meadows, the lanes,
The guildhalls, the carved choirs.
There'll be books; it will linger on
In galleries; but all that remains
For us will be concrete and tyres
Most things are never meant.
This won't be, most likely: but greeds
And garbage are too thick-strewn
To be swept up now, or invent
Excuses that make them all needs.
I just think it will happen, soon.'
(Philip Larkin, *Going, Going*)

Although in the West we may have advanced materially or technologically down the past two centuries (in agriculture, industry, medicine, surgery, domestic appliances, communications, transport, etc) these advancements have not brought about a corresponding spiritual advance, or increased humankind's poetic and artistic sensibilities. It is quite surprising to discover that in the so-called 'Dark' Ages in Europe, and in the much-despised medieval period, people possessed as much, if not more, spirituality, as much awareness of the beauties of wild nature, and as much poetic sensibility as we possess them today. This can be shown by quoting the following beautiful and sublime poetry, written in those far off times:

Sliabh gCua [pronounced slliav gua]
'Sliabh gCua, haunt of wolves, rugged and dark, the wind wails about its glens, wolves howl around its chasms; the fierce brown deer bells in autumn around it, the crane screams over its crags.'
(Irish, author unknown, 9th Century)

Deirdre Remembers a Scottish Glen.
'Glen of fruit and fish and pools, its peaked hills of loveliest wheat, it is distressful for me to think of it – glen of bees, of long-horned wild oxen.

Glen of cuckoos and thrushes and blackbirds, precious is its cover to every fox, glen of wild garlic and watercress, of woods, of shamrock and flowers, leafy and twisting-crested.

Sweet are the cries of the brown-backed dappled deer under the oakwood above the bare hill-tops, gentle hinds that are timid lying hidden in the great-treed glen.

Glen of the rowans with scarlet berries, with fruit fit for every flock of birds, a slumbrous paradise for the badger in their quiet burrows with their young.

Glen of the blue-eyed vigorous hawks, glen abounding
in every harvest, glen of the ridged and pointed peaks,
of blackberries and sloes and apples.

Glen of the sleek brown round-faced otters that are
pleasant and active in fishing, many are the white-winged
stately swans, and salmon breeding along the rocky bank.

Glen of the tangled branching yews, dewy glen with
level lawn of kine, chalk-white starry sunny glen,
glen of graceful pearl-like high-bred women.'
(Irish, author unknown, 14th century)

Pangur Ban.
'I and Pangur Ban my cat
'Tis a like task we are at
Hunting mice is his delight,
Hunting words I sit at night.
Better far than praise of men
'Tis to sit with book and pen;
Pangur bears me no ill-will
He too plies his simple skill.
Oftentimes a mouse will stray
In the hero Pangur's way;
Oftentimes my keen thought set
Takes a meaning in its net.
'Gainst the wall he sets his eye
Full and fierce and sharp and sly;
'Gainst the wall of knowledge I
All my little wisdom try.
Practice every day has made
Pangur perfect in his trade;
I get wisdom day and night
Turning darkness into light.'
(Written by a ninth century Irish monk in St. Gallen, Switzerland)

Chapter Thirty-Seven

Ignorance and Wealth

When politicians and leaders in our supposedly highly advanced, democratic, free market Western (or Westernised) systems blather on about our 'freedoms', what 'freedoms' are they actually referring to in their self-deluded, or indeed cynical, minds? Not the freedom for a higher, better, or more beautiful spiritual or artistic or poetic or earth-centred life, but rather the freedom to be greedy, to be selfish, to 'get and spend', to acquire ever more material goods for ourselves, to economically compete with each other, to vote for mediocre politicians and their self-serving, technologically-fixated, false ideals, and the freedom to conform to profit-making businesses and bureaucratic organisations.

Charles Darwin's Theory of Evolution, natural selection and the supposed 'survival of the fittest', seems to rather conveniently fit in with the needs of a capitalist society, and at present seems to be the generally held belief in the Western world, but is it the whole truth? The Russian author, Prince Peter Kropotkin, rejected Social Darwinism as a Western ploy which seems to have led to the Western world's harsh individualism and self-seeking capitalism, and he showed that evolution just as easily produces mutually beneficial co-operation between animals, as well as between humans in 'primitive' societies. It seems that nature is not always 'red in tooth and claw' nor are primitive peoples always 'savage' and 'barbaric', but modern Western society can be even more cruel and unjust and selfish than either animals or non-Western cultures.

'...Where ignorance and wealth their course pursue,
Each tree must tumble down – old 'Lea-Close Oak', adieu.'
(John Clare, *The Village Minstrel*, 1821)

'I think that I shall never see
A billboard lovely as a tree.
Perhaps unless the billboards fall,
I'll never see a tree at all.'
(Ogden Nash)

'Greed, paralysed imaginations, and a dotty lust for some vague, shabby modernity will go on destroying. Rich, influential pigs do behave in this way, and will go on destroying so that they can put up hideous pens for other hopeful, happy pigs to work in.'
(John Osborne)

'The flower-fed buffaloes of the spring
In the days of long ago,
Ranged where the locomotives sing
And the prairie flowers lie low:-
The tossing, blooming, perfumed grass
Is swept away by the wheat,
Wheels and wheels and wheels spin by
In the spring that still is sweet.
But the flower-fed buffaloes of the spring
Left us, long ago.
They gore no more, they bellow no more,
They trundle around the hills no more:-
With the Blackfeet, lying low,
With the Pawnees, lying low,
Lying low.'
(Vachel Lindsay, *The Flower-fed Buffaloes*)

Chapter Thirty-Eight

The End of History

The writer and philosopher Rousseau stated over two centuries ago that 'Man is born free, but is everywhere in chains', and that statement is as true today as it was when Rousseau observed the oppression and repression that mankind inflicts on himself and others of his own species in the Western 'civilised' nations in his times. Since Rousseau's time, and in no small part due to the ideas of democracy, education and political liberalism, as espoused by philosophical revolutionaries such as Rousseau, the tyrannical oppression of the Church and the Landed Gentry has been dismantled, yet in many ways the aristocrats and the priests have been replaced by the oppressive tyranny of the State and Big Business, in our bureaucratic, conformist, image-conscious, competitive, materialistic, consumerist, manipulative, and exploitative Western (or Westernised) capitalist nation-states, of which Singapore is the 'shining' example. As if successfully competing with each other globally on the so-called free market (actually highly controlled by the privileged elite) is the sum total and goal of humankind's existence and long evolution on this planet!

In a so-called 'free market' economy our existence is measured in terms of 'getting and spending', how we are indulging our fancies and whims in purchasing consumer goods, or by passively viewing mass entertainments. Everything is measured and weighed in a monetary or cynically utilitarian way, as an economic 'resource', a consumer 'product', a leisure 'facility', a genetic 'bank', a tourist 'resort', etc.

Scientific 'progress' and capitalism are the presiding gods or rather idols of the modern world, gods in an abstract sense, as opposed to a living or a vital sense, but idols nonetheless. Our temporal as well as spiritual needs are now satisfied through scientific knowledge, business, shopping, mass tourism, and mass entertainments, in the same way that a medieval knight satisfied his spiritual and temporal needs through the Court, the Church, the Christian God, and through Military Glory (the idols have changed but not the process).

Science and the global free market are not the 'end of history', the final summation and glory of humankind's evolution and long history. Science, industry and capitalism have indeed achieved great improvements in material prosperity for a large section of the population of the Western world, but have that affluence and prosperity improved humankind's basic nature, and has it really created a kinder, wiser, more humane, more compassionate, more creative, or more noble order of being on this planet? Or does such 'progress' produce greedier, lazier, more selfish, more uncaring, more self-indulgent, more self-seeking, shallower, vainer and more vacuous individuals? Are we pandering to our 'greeds' rather than to our needs in the modern Western world? Even as far as our democratic system is concerned, we do not necessarily make the wisest or the most ethical choices, since the general public can be swayed one way or another through self-interest, greed, propaganda, popular pressure and the dissemination of half-truths by the privileged elite, by politicians and by their spin-doctors.

It seems as if our modern, Western, urbanised, industrialised, technologically obsessed, scientifically reductionist, materialist societies are turning us into money-making automatons, consumer robots, soulless, almost insect-like creatures programmed by the system to become branded, packaged, standardised, marketed, synthetic, disinfected, mass produced, homogenised, digitalised, pre-fabricated, pre-determined and purposeful. Could we find not even a little space in this capitalised world for undomesticated, untamed, uncultivated, uncontrolled and unprofitable (in purely materialistic terms) wild nature? It is simply not enough for wild nature to be corralled in small, scattered nature reserves, or far-flung national or state parks, but nature should be part-and-parcel of our everyday existence, both within and beyond the city's walled garden: God grant the day when humankind lives in better harmony with nature and the Earth, 'not for idle sport or food, but for inspiration and our own true recreation', (George Catlin)

Nature is not merely an economic, medicinal, academic, recreational or scientific 'resource' for consumption and dissection, but it is also a source of wonder, of inspiration, of beauty, of poetry and of art. Nature conservation and wildlife preservation are often of themselves economically unsound (in the short-term), unprofitable in a materialist sense, and seem downright useless in a utilitarian world. Yet humankind needs nature to evoke his poetic, artistic and spiritual sensibilities, and to reawaken his sense of 'connection' between himself and the Creation. Nature is harsh, brutal, cruel, rough and chaotic, yet she is also kind, considerate, benign, ordered and balanced, and that is the very reason why nature should be preserved, as an antidote to our stifling, cultivated, controlled, categorised, systemised, corporate, efficient, hygienic, comfortable, self-constrained, urbanised, house-bound, and bourgeois way of life.

Only a self-deluded Luddite could really wish to return or go back to a primitive, non-technological, harsh, pre-industrial existence – else why has humankind spent the past four thousand years strenuously trying to free itself from nature's circumscribed and insecure conditions? But that does not mean we should shut ourselves completely away from nature's inspiration (poetic, artistic or spiritual), or see nature as just a 'resource' for consumption, recreation or dissection.

The Ancient World appears to have had a far better and wiser concept of nature, though of course forests were felled, and wild animals were killed for sport, for profit and for entertainment. Yet the Ancient Greeks, the Ancient Romans, the Ancient Chinese and other civilisations (particularly the empire of King Asoka in Ancient India) were quite conscious of humankind's destruction of the natural world many thousands of years ago. Reading some of the literary works from the Ancient World (such as the writings of Pliny the Elder, Virgil, Ovid, Lao-Tzu, and the Ancient Indian Vedas and epics) it appears the Ancients saw the Earth as a living and vital thing, as opposed to the modern, Western, scientific, mechanistic concept of the earth as merely dead matter. The view of the Ancient philosophers toward nature was a healthy blend of nature mysticism, of poetic and artistic appreciation, of spirituality, as well as of emotionally detached science and objectivity. Modern man has gone too far down the road of mechanistic science, and as a result we have become too detached – mentally, emotionally, spiritually, and artistically – from nature and the living, vital Earth. In the words of the author and naturalist Henry Beston (1888-1968), 'We need another and a wiser and perhaps a more mystical concept of animals.' (Beston, *The Outermost House*)

Not that the light of nature mysticism and compassion towards the 'lower' creatures and the living Earth has ever become entirely extinguished, even though it may merely have flickered through certain eras. Even in the Dark Ages and in the Middle Ages, which we view today as brutal, backward and ignorant times, it is possible to discover certain enlightened individuals who had a deep concern for the Earth and the Creation. For example, Saint Cuthbert, who established a wildlife sanctuary on the Farne Islands off the Northumbrian coastline of England; or the Italian Saint Francis of Assisi, who reverenced all of God's Creation, even the animals and the birds, and whom the bird-slaughtering modern Italians have apparently forgotten; and the falconer and medieval authority on bird life, Emperor Frederick the Second, who was called 'Stupor Mundi' (the 'Wonder of the World') by his contemporaries for his deep knowledge on all matters, and particularly natural history and falconry.

Chapter Thirty-Nine

A Sordid Shilling

In the Western, materialist world too many scientists and politicians have submitted to that abominable, murderous doctrine of mechanistic nature originally presented to the world by the brutal philosophy of Descartes, and which has filtered down into the popular consciousness. It is not the animals which have no feelings or souls, but the mechanistic scientists and vivisectionists, puffed up with ego, intellect and conceit, who have given their souls and feelings away for a sordid shilling.

Nor is nature conservation and wildlife preservation a self-indulgent luxury, only affordable to developed nations, since the concept of reverence for the Creation and for the preservation of natural resources is as old as humankind, and can be found both as an idea and as a practice in every culture in world history, more or less, whether 'primitive' or 'advanced'. Even the wild, often cruel and brutal gauchos of the Argentine pampas in the nineteenth century viewed the Italian immigrants with utter contempt when they saw them indiscriminately slaughtering wild birds purely for 'sport' (this is described by W.H. Hudson in Chapter One of his book *Adventures Among Birds*).

There is really no excuse for cruelty and indiscriminate killing of wild animals, whether through greed, blood lust, ignorance or indifference. Moreover, since animals are, arguably, lower or lesser than mankind, morally, intellectually, spiritually or whatever, then we should treat them with compassion, since we should know better than they do and have been given the moral choice to do good, which they have not. Yet, on the other hand, maybe reverence for nature and the Earth is after all merely a 'silly little love of nature', just a pastime or a hobby or an interest or a whim, to be done just occasionally, and as a temporary escape and a refuge from the city and from suburban life, since that is how most people live today: in the walled garden of civilisation. But it is undoubtedly true that modern, Western man has gone too far in the direction of trim, tidy, chemically cleansed, tamed, city-bred, house-bound, and corporate life.

'This may be regarded as the mental attitude of the wild man from the woods, but something may be said for it. Sir Walter Raleigh explained, centuries ago, the reason of our desire for and pleasure in trim gardens, lawns, parks, and neatly cut hedges of box and privet and holly: those surroundings of the house were invented as a refuge from the harsh, brambly outside wilderness, the stinging nettles, scratching thorns, sharp hurtful stones and hidden pits – from all the roughnesses and general horriblenesses of an incult Nature.

'But that's all a feeling of long ago, it may be answered; it has gone out now, and we have come back to Nature – the dear old beautiful mother! Have we indeed? Lawns have not gone out; on the contrary, it appears to me that the idea of the lawn, like the idea of clothes, has entered into our souls and manifests itself more and more in all our surroundings, our dwellings, our persons, our habits…And if Sir Walter Raleigh himself were to return to us in all his glory and splendour, and if someone, opening the History of the World, should read that passage about lawns to him, I think he would cry out: "Oh, but you have now gone too far in that direction! Your rooms, your tables, all the thousand appointments of your establishment, your own appearance, your hard-scraped skins, your conversation suffocate me. Let me out – let me go back to the place I came from!"

'What then of all the beautiful things we say of Nature? it may be asked. Why, only this: it amounts to as much as all the beautiful things we say about painted pictures, jewels, tapestries, old lace, Chippendale furniture, and what not. We are not in Nature; we are out of her, having made our own conditions, and our conditions have reacted upon and made us what we are – artificial creatures. Nature is now something pretty to go and look at occasionally, but not too often, nor for too long a time.' (W. H. Hudson, *The Book of a Naturalist*)

Modern, Western man lives today in a functionalist, materialist, technologically obsessed, scientifically reductionist era. Our clothes are utilitarian, our architecture is utilitarian, as are our transport systems, our cities, our streets, in fact our whole way of life. We have become utilitarian, standardised, homogenised, scientific and deadly dull. Where can one find today the beauty, elegance and grace of the eighteenth century, when one looks at the clothes they wore, their architecture (whether rustic or urban), their stately homes and landscaped gardens, or, on the contrary, old paintings and photographs of wild, painted, picturesque 'savages' (such as those magnificent portraits of Native American Indians in their traditional costumes by George Catlin).

We modern, corporate Westerners have become homogenised, vulgarian, materialistic, technocratic, petit-bourgeois philistines, and we have forgotten the 'empire of the imagination' or reverence for wild nature, for the picturesque, for Gothic architecture, for '...twilight groves, and dusky caves, Long-sounding aisles, and intermingled graves.' (Alexander Pope) Dreams, visions and the imagination are far from trivial pursuits. The author Horace Walpole saw the wisdom of visions long ago when he stated, 'Visions, you know, have always been my pasture; and so far from growing old enough to quarrel with their emptiness, I almost think there is no wisdom comparable to that of exchanging what is called the realities of life for dreams. Old castles, old pictures, old histories, and the babble of old people, make one live back into centuries that cannot disappoint one. One holds fast and surely what is past.' (Horace Walpole, 1766)

Liberal, democratic, parliamentary democracy as well as state socialism are functional, utilitarian, materialist systems, and hence they will produce functionalist, materialist, utilitarian people and a functionalist, materialist, utilitarian environment. We modern Westerners bow down before the dull, utilitarian, conformist tyranny of our era, that is, the scientific, materialist philosophy of life. Would those elegant and ornate stately homes and those graceful Georgian terraces have been built in a social democracy, probably not, since they were not built for the petit-bourgeois or for the 'common' people, but for a small, cultured, exclusive, aristocratic elite, however unfair and unjust such a system undoubtedly was! Art, beauty and nature are utterly unproductive, useless and uneconomical in a purely utilitarian, capitalist or socialist way, since they do not provide for our physical wants, our materialistic economic productivity, and hardly even satisfy our material comforts, yet they are nevertheless a necessity of life, because humankind has been given an aesthetic and spiritual sensibility.

When people unthinkingly talk about 'progress' and 'development' what are they actually referring to? Are they referring to progress and development in art, in aesthetic sensibility, in awareness of or reverence for the natural world and the Earth? Or are they just referring to advances in material comforts and in luxuries, in scientific inventions and in ever more technological sophistication? Industry and technology have undoubtedly provided the West with many material luxuries, but have they bettered the human soul, or given us a more beautiful environment to inhabit? When we compare beautiful and ornate eighteenth-century architecture and old, timber-framed, rustic cottages with modernist, brutalist, functionalist, monolithic, concrete, steel or glass office-blocks, and then remember that lovely old buildings were demolished, even entire streets swept away, to build such monstrosities, then the lie of 'progress' is truly exposed (that is, the building of hideous pens by the privileged elite for happy pigs to work in, in the words of the writer John Osborne[6]). Take a look at old shop frontages, old lamp posts, old churches, old cathedrals, old country estates, old books, old manuscripts, old costumes, old paintings, old furniture, and compare these objects and artefacts to modern mass-produced, standardised products, and ask where all our 'progress' has led us. At the beginning of our technocratic, industrialised, scientific, materialist and machine age the artist and Gothic architect Augustus Welby Pugin wisely wished to 'pluck from the age the mask of superior attainments so falsely assumed, and…to direct the attention of all back to the real merit of a past and better day' (which might just as easily be said about the conceit of the modern twenty-first-century world, as of the conceit of the rapidly industrialising world of Victorian England in Pugin's day).

---

[6] In England in the 1960s and in the 1970s many fine old city centres, market town high streets and village high streets were demolished almost wholescale and redeveloped. Quaint and handsome Victorian, Georgian, and even medieval buildings (which could have been renovated, or were in a good state of preservation) were unnecessarily demolished. Most of the so-called 're-developments' consisted of soulless office-blocks, characterless shopping malls, and ring roads. But how can replacing buildings of high architectural quality, craftsmanship, elegance, grace, individuality, and historical value with buildings of low value (characterless, pre-fabricated, 'rabbit hutches') be considered a 'development' rather than a degeneration?! Or is the idea of 'progress' and 'development' merely an excuse to cover up greed, ignorance, ruthlessness, venality, philistinism, economic cold-bloodedness, and cultural vandalism? As John Osborne points out, 'Greed, paralysed imaginations, and a dotty lust for some vague, shabby modernity will go on destroying. Rich, influential pigs do behave in this way, and will go on destroying so that they can put up hideous pens for other hopeful, happy pigs to work in.'

Is modern, Western man really so much freer and wiser and more aesthetically intelligent than previous generations, or non-Western cultures? Is Western man really the best and wisest and highest representative of Homo sapiens in world history? In any case, what does such freedom mean in the modern world of consumerism and materialism, than just the freedom to 'get and spend', to exploit and to plunder natural resources, to be greedy, to be selfish, to be smug, and to conform to bourgeois values. Are we modern Westerners any more artistically gifted or spiritually wiser than previous generations? There have always been creative artists, writers, poets, eccentrics, sages and mystics in every generation and in every land throughout recorded time: the Romantics of the late eighteenth and early nineteenth centuries, medieval alchemists, astrologers and magicians, Jewish Cabbalists, the Celtic Druids (such as the legendary Merlin), Greco-Roman philosophers and natural scientists (such as the Stoics and the Pythagoreans), the Zoroastrians (of Ancient Persia), the Islamic Sufis, the Old Testament Prophets, the Buddha, Confucius, Lao-Tzu, Sitting Bull, and Mahavira of India (the founder of Jainism).The Ancient World, and 'primitive' peoples, had a certain wisdom which we have almost lost today in our progressive, forward-looking Western world because 'the Ancients knew how Nature is a dark Room, and that is why their plays will stand when even our Playhouses are crumbled into Dust: for their Tragedy reflects Corruption and men are the same now as they have ever been.' (Peter Ackroyd, *Hawksmoor*)

It appears that modern, Western man has been almost entirely overpowered by the materialistic, secular, utilitarian, functionalist, highly controlled, scientifically reductionist, unimaginative, and technocratic Spirit of the Age. This contemporary zeitgeist of the modern, Western world is spreading all over the globe, and many countries now are seeking to adopt the Western way, because if they do not they will become losers in the global economy. But what do all of the West's comforts and luxuries actually amount to, if nature is poisoned and degraded in the process of commercial self-gain, and if our hearts and souls are crushed beneath industrialism, reductionism, and technological materialism. The price of uncontrolled technological progress and materialist philosophies is a degraded, denuded and polluted world: plastics, sprawling soulless suburbia, brutalist and functionalist architecture, motorways, barbed wire, factories, industrial estates, power stations, electricity pylons, agricultural and industrial chemicals, flotsam in the seas and effluvia in the rivers.

We modern Westerners have become too city bred, house bound, corporate, homogenised, chemically scrubbed and cleansed, scientific, functional and artificial. The modern Western world has lost its primitive, wild, romantic charm, its spontaneity of human feeling, its imaginative powers, and any awareness of, or correspondence with, the natural world. The floral monstrosities and arboreal freaks we see planted in our parks and gardens are glaring examples of the modern world's unnaturalness and artificiality, '...that over-culture which reminds one by its broad glare, its stiffness, and heaviness of the double daisies of the garden, compared with their modest and sensitive kindred of the fields.' (William Wordsworth) Science and technology have gone too far in their domination of the human spirit and the natural world. We must leave some space on the Earth for the spontaneity of wild nature, and also some space in our own hearts and souls for unscientific, non-dogmatic, non-reductionist dreams and visions.

We have dismantled from our souls in the secular Western world the dogmatic chains of the Church and religion, only to see those chains now replaced by the dogmatic shackles of science and reductionist materialism. We modern Westerners shackle ourselves to a soulless, artificial, invented, over-intellectualised, coldly logical, non-poetical, scientifically reductionist world-view. We are striving after greater and better science and technology, thinking that they will of themselves lead humankind to a new, glorious, utopian Golden Age of peace, prosperity and immortality, yet always just in the future!

Uncontrolled science, technology and rampant consumer capitalism will not lead humankind to a glorious golden future, but will only lead to gross materialism, technocratic wealth (for the privileged elite), and wasteful extravagance of our human as well as our finite natural resources.

'...One impulse from a vernal wood
May teach you more of man,
Of moral evil and of good,
Than all the sages can.

Sweet is the lore which Nature brings;
Our meddling intellect

Mis-shapes the beauteous forms of things:-
We murder to dissect.

Enough of Science and of Art;
Close up those barren leaves;
Come forth, and bring with you a heart
That watches and receives.'
(William Wordsworth, from *The Tables Turned*)

'...science and rationality are limited in the truths they can reveal. In fact, they are virtually blind; they explain nothing. And all around us lies a great unseen mystery. Omnia exeunt in mysterium [all ends in mystery].' (Arthur Machen)

Chapter Forty

Beside the Immortals

The eternity and infinity of nature cannot always be present to the human soul at all times, since humankind needs to attend also to its purely physical or biological requirements. Yet it is also important for humankind to experience, if only occasionally, the eternity of nature, and our place in the greater scheme of things, in order to remind us of our place in the web of all life and of the Creation. This mystical sensation, which seems to be a kind of loss of ego and a regression to the wonders of childhood, an absorption of the soul into the greater whole of Creation, can be discovered in certain works of art or literature which call for a return to nature and to a child-like simplicity of outlook, of wonderment, and of an imaginative relationship to the world of things. For example, in the paintings of Samuel Palmer (particularly in *The Waterfalls, Pistil Mawddach, North Wales*, 1835/6; *Hilly Scene with Church and Moon*, c.1826/7; and *Cornfield by Moonlight, with the Evening Star*, c.1826/7); in Philipp Otto Runge's painting entitled *Child in the Meadow*[7]; in the paintings of Caspar David Friedrich; in the paintings of Paul Nash (such as *Landscape of the Summer Solstice*, 1943); and in the literary works of Thomas Traherne, W.H. Hudson, William Wordsworth, William

---

[7] This is a painting which evokes the same feelings of wonderment at the beauty and mystery of birth and life as William Wordsworth's poem *Ode on Intimations of Immortality*:
'Our birth is but a sleep and a forgetting;
The Soul that rises with us, our life's Star
Hath had elsewhere its setting
And cometh from afar;
Not in entire forgetfulness,
And not in utter nakedness,
But trailing clouds of glory do we come...'

Blake, Richard Jefferies, Thomas Gray, Algernon Blackwood, and John Clare.

'Nature then...
To me was all in all – I cannot paint
What then I was. The sounding cataract
Haunted me like a passion: the tall rock,
The mountain, and the deep and gloomy wood,
Their colours and their forms, were then to me
An appetite: a feeling and a love
That had no need of a remoter charm.'
  (William Wordsworth)

Mouse's Nest.
'I found a ball of grass among the hay
And progged it as I passed and went away;
And when I looked I fancied something stirred,
And turned agen and hoped to catch the bird –
When out an old mouse bolted in the wheats
With all her young ones hanging at her teats;
She looked so odd and so grotesque to me,
I ran and wondered what the thing could be,
And pushed the knapweed bunches where I stood;
Then the mouse hurried from the craking brood.
The young ones squeaked, and as I went away
She found her nest again among the hay.
The water o'er the pebbles scarce could run
And broad old cesspools glittered in the sun.'
(John Clare)

'To see a World in a Grain of Sand
And a Heaven in a Wild Flower,
Hold Infinity in the palm of your hand
And Eternity in an hour.'
(William Blake, *Auguries of Innocence*)

'It is enough to lie on the sward in the shadow of green boughs, to listen to the songs of summer, to drink in the sunlight, the air, the flowers, the sky, the beauty of all. Or upon the hilltops to watch the white-clouds rising over the curved hill-lines, their shadows descending the slope. Or on the beach to listen to the sweet sigh as the smooth sea runs up and recedes. It is lying beside the immortals, indrawing the life of the ocean, the earth, and the sun. I want always to be in company with these, with earth, and sun, and sea, and stars by night. The pettiness of house-life – chairs and tables – and the pettiness of observances, the petty necessity of useless labour, useless because productive of nothing, chafe me the year through. I want to be always in company with the sun, and sea, and earth. These, and the stars by night, are my natural companions.'

(Richard Jefferies, *Story of my Heart*).

'Leaves from eternity are simple things
To the world's gaze – whereto a spirit clings
Sublime and lasting. Trampled under foot,
The daisy lives, and strikes its little root
Into the lap of time: centuries may come,
And pass away into the silent tomb,
And still the child, hid in the womb of time,
Shall smile and pluck them when this simple rhyme
Shall be forgotten, like a churchyard stone,
Or lingering lie unnoticed and alone.
When eighteen hundred years, our common date,
Grow many thousands in their marching state,
Ay, still the child, with pleasure in his eye,
Shall cry – the daisy! A familiar cry –
And run to pluck it, in the self-same state
As when Time found it in his infant date;
And, like a child himself, when all was new,
Might smile with wonder, and take notice too…
Spring and autumnal years shall bloom, and fade,
Longer than songs that poets ever made…'
(John Clare, *The Eternity of Nature*)

'The meanest flowret of the vale
The simplest note that swells the gale,
The common sun, the air, the skies,
To him are opening paradise.'
(Thomas Gray)

'We may say that impressions are vivid and live vividly in the mind, even to the end of life, in those alone in whom something that is of the child survives in the adult – the measureless delight in all this visible world, experienced every day by the millions of children happily born outside the city's gates, but so rarely expressed in literature, as Traherne, let us say, expressed it; and with the delight, the sense of wonder in all life, which is akin to, if not one with, the mythical faculty, and if experienced in a high degree is a sense of the supernatural in all natural things. We may say, in fact, that unless the soul goes out to meet what we see we do not see it; nothing do we see, not a beetle, not a blade of grass.'

(W.H. Hudson, *The Book of a Naturalist*)

'[To know] again the feelings of those early days when "A boy's will is the wind's will, And the thoughts of youth are long, long thoughts", when all the world smells sweet and golden as a summer's day, and a village street is endless as the sky.'
(Algernon Blackwood, *The Centaur*)

'...I have felt
A presence that disturbs me with the joy
Of elevated thoughts; a sense sublime
Of something far more deeply interfused,
Whose dwelling is the light of setting suns,
And the round ocean and the living air,
And the blue sky, and in the mind of man:
A motion and a spirit, that impels
All thinking things, all objects of all thought,
And rolls through all things. Therefore am I still
A lover of the meadows and the woods,
And mountains; and of all that we behold
From this green earth...'
(William Wordsworth, *Tintern Abbey*)

Chapter Forty-One

A Dead and Sterile World

Scientific reductionism, empiricism, technological materialism, reason, logic, pure intellect and our modern urbanised, indoor way of life, all combine to create a dead and sterile world. Yet this world is neither sterile, dead nor machine-like, but a living and a vital thing. The so-clever and so-conceited scientists and technologists who are seeking after a chemical reaction, a mathematical formula, a dogmatic set of physical laws, or a 'Big Bang' hypothesis, to explain away the wonder, mystery, nature, or origin of the universe, are a bunch of blind, soulless pedants, since the answers to all these questions, lie both within as well as outside the human mind and soul. Wise men can only wonder at the beauty and ultimate mystery of the universe, and dream dreams with the poets and the mystics.

'...Wise men in tracing Nature's laws
Ascend unto the highest Cause;
Shepherds with humble fearfulness
Walk safely, though their light be life:
Though wise men better know the way
It seems no honest heart can stray.

There is no merit in the wise
But Love, (the shepherd's sacrifice);
Wise men, all ways of knowledge past,
To the shepherd's wonder come at last:
To know can only wonder breed,
And not to know is wonder's seed...'
(Sidney Godolphin)

Roots.
'I've known days when a passing sight

Was window to the infinite.
There is a place where a cart track
Cuts deep into a green down's back,
As wire cuts cheese, and you may walk
In shade between two walls of chalk,
Save at sun's height. Once in noon glare
I came on sudden shadow there,
And looking up I saw on high
A tree whose branches brushed the sky
Sprouting from the cliff-edge and, wonder!
A tree inverted, branching under
Into the chalk. It was as if
Twin seeds had struck root on the cliff,
And one grown skyward and one thirled
His fingers to the underworld;
But those down-delving limbs and shoots
Were that same lofty giant's roots.

Through the cleft ridge the pathway led
Down to a vale with trees o'erspread,
But for a while I scarce could see
In all that vale a single tree,
Only roots, roots...Then the path wound
Upwards; I footed open ground
And shadowless grass, but I was 'ware
Of a power moving in the air,
A ferment underneath the green,
Under each tree a tree unseen.
And when a scared bird rose to fly,
His outspread wings against the sky
Seemed roots. Methought, all Nature bruits
A mystery. O what the roots
And on what stem eternal grows
Earth's evanescent sunset rose?
And when the crimson fades in gloom
Darkness bursts into starry bloom,
And globed buds the heavens fill
Rooted more deep than Igdrasil.'
(Thomas Sharp)

The modern Western concept of 'progress' in a linear direction down the centuries, from 'savage' to 'civilised', from inferior to superior, from backward to advanced, is a myth, a fantasy, a delusion and a conceit, since life itself is cyclical. Yet it cannot be denied that the West is advancing in technological sophistication, and in a lifestyle of ever increasing consumerism and convenience (or at least for a certain privileged section of humankind), but are we really advancing artistically, intellectually, aesthetically and spiritually as a species?

Materialism and technological progress are literally costing us the earth, degrading and denuding the natural world, yet humankind needs nature and the wild because it has been given an aesthetic and spiritual sensibility, which nature helps to bring forth. People in the Ancient World and in the Middle Ages – before the huge material advances of science and materialism – lived closer to nature, to the Earth, to the natural seasons, to the rhythm and the cycle of life, and to the Anima Mundi (the 'World Soul', or the living, universal Spirit of Nature), even though many may have lived hard lives (or at least many of the serfs and the peasants, though on the plus side that life was rich in community and spirituality). And the Ancient and medieval worlds produced the most subliminal works of art: beautiful churches, magnificent cathedrals, illuminated manuscripts, wonderful tapestries, not to mention the awe-inspiring temples and pyramids of the Ancient World. Much of modern art, on the other hand, seems rather self-indulgent, bourgeois, self-referential, and pretentious in comparison with the sheer magnificence and beauty of medieval and ancient art, which was not created for money, or for individual fame, or for mere showiness and entertainment, or to boost the artist's ego (as much of modern art seems to be), but for the greater glory of God, or for the gods, or for the Pope (who was God's Ambassador on Earth) or for the Emperor or King, who ruled by Divine Right.

We modern Westerners did not invent or discover scientific, technological, intellectual and spiritual knowledge, since most of our basic knowledge (about the world and the universe) we inherited (or re-discovered during the Renaissance in Europe) from the Ancient Greeks and the Ancient Romans, who in their turn got it from the Ancient Egyptians, the Ancient Babylonians, the Ancient Indians and the Ancient Oriental peoples, who in their turn acquired it from some unknown civilisation, maybe even the mythical Atlanteans and Lemurians (who knows?). Yet, is all knowledge acquired only through the intellect and by scientific empiricism, or is there also a 'divine' knowledge, which is spiritual, intuitive, or inborn in the human soul? A hard, poverty-stricken, or rural existence does not necessarily produce stupid, brutal or ignorant people, since some very creative individuals had terrible, deprived, or isolated childhoods, yet were self-taught and managed to produce some of the world's greatest artistic works. For example, the poetry of John Clare, George Crabbe, Robbie Burns and Robert Bloomfield (who all grew up in poor, isolated rural communities), and the literary works of Maxim Gorky (who endured a wretched childhood in Russia).

Are we modern, affluent, technologically sophisticated Westerners all 'striving after comforts that bring no comfort to the heart' in our acquisitive, competitive, materialistic, harshly individualistic, technocratic, utilitarian societies? Yet it cannot be denied that there is at least a greater awareness among the general population concerning humankind's degradation of the Earth, and its unhealthy consequences for all of humankind. Upon that foundation alone it is to be hoped that future generations will learn to live in better harmony with the natural world.

There is a divine cord that runs throughout history and which can never be entirely severed or broken, even in the most barbaric or rationalistic of ages, and that cord is nature mysticism, a 'divine' knowledge acquired via the soul and the senses, which binds humankind to this earth, our living mother, and which is no fad or whim or foolish sentimentality, since the Earth is our Home.

'Oh nature! all sufficient, over all,
Enrich me with the knowledge of thy
Works.'
(Author unknown, Ancient Roman writer)

Nature mystics and nature poets have existed in every generation and in every land throughout humankind's history, and they did not seek knowledge and truth exclusively in the material or in the intellectual worlds, or exclusively through technological 'progress', but through natural or divine laws, through intuition, through Nature's universal Truths, through a selfless identification with nature, and through 'books in brooks and sermons in stones' (in the words of William Wordsworth).

A Snowy Winter's Day.
'Beneath a fleece of Winter white
The seeds of Spring are shut up tight,

Waiting for a milder hour
To burst again, bear fruit and flower;
Though flower will wither and soon decline
Seeds are sown to renew the line.
Though Life is short and quickly passed
Nature's Great Mystery forever lasts.'
(Matthew Irwin)

To the Utilitarians
'Avaunt this economic rage!
What would it bring? – an iron age,
When Fact with heartless search explored
Shall be Imagination's Lord,
And sway with absolute control
The god-like functions of the Soul.
Not thus can knowledge elevate
Our Nature from her fallen state.
With sober Reason Faith unites
To vindicate the ideal rights
Of Human-Kind – the true agreeing
Of objects with internal seeing,
Of effort with the end of Being.'
(William Wordsworth)

'Man Brings All that he has or can have Into the World with him.
Man is Born like a Garden ready Planted and Sown.' (William Blake)

The only true progress is a kind of regression, a regression to the
wonder of childhood and a going back, or rather forward, to Nature.
To the cynical and the world-weary adult the Earth appears dull,
corrupt, devious, cruel, competitive, and even ugly, but to the
uncorrupted child '…like a land of dreams, so various, so beautiful, so
new…' (Matthew Arnold)

There are things on this Earth, and mystical sensations, which
reason, science, logic, the intellect, and book learning will never
comprehend:
'A wild weird clime that lieth, sublime,
Out of Space – out of Time.'
(Edgar Allen Poe)

The American author Henry Miller in his book *Tropic of Capricorn* perfectly illustrates the difference between the selfishness and cynicism of modern, 'civilised' societies and the selflessness and generosity of so-called 'primitive' societies, in the following passage, where he discusses his 'mentally disadvantaged' sister in the 'civilised' society of America:

'The mother from whose loins I sprang was a complete stranger to me. To begin with, after giving birth to me she gave birth to my sister, whom I usually refer to as my brother. My sister was a sort of harmless monster, an angel who had been given the body of an idiot. It gave me a strange feeling, as a boy, to be growing up and developing side by side with this being who was doomed to remain all her life a mental dwarf. It was impossible to be a brother to her because it was impossible to regard this atavistic hulk of a body as a "sister". She would have functioned perfectly, I imagine, among the Australian primitives. She might even have been raised to power and eminence among them, for, as I said, she was the essence of goodness, she knew no evil. But so far as living the civilised life goes she was helpless; she not only had no desire to kill but she had no desire to thrive at the expense of others. She was incapacitated for work, because even if they had been able to train her to make caps for high explosives, for example, she might absent-mindedly throw her wages in the river on the way home or she might give them to a beggar in the street. Often in my presence she was whipped like a dog for having performed some beautiful act of grace in her absent-mindedness, as they called it. Nothing was worse, I learned as a child, than to do a good deed without reason. I had received the same punishment as my sister, in the beginning, because I too had a habit of giving things away, especially new things which had just been given me...'

As the nineteenth-century American senator Henry Dawes stated so perspicaciously, *selfishness lies at the bottom of civilisation,* not generosity or selflessness or kindness or community- spiritedness, and that is why the Native Americans and the 'primitive' peoples had to go, have to go, along with human decency, and angelic 'idiots' like Henry Miller's sister, in our modern, venal, corrupt, capitalistic, civilised, 'free market', Social Darwinist global village. But, hey, that's progress, folks.

Chapter Forty-Two

Longevity and Learning

The earth and its bountiful nature are being spoiled and degraded by technocratic, materialist philosophies. The question now facing humankind is this: do we want a living, vital world which respects the natural world and the creative human imagination, or, on the other hand, a grossly materialistic, scientifically rational, reductive, chemically poisoned, culturally homogenised, dead, and mechanistic world? Is our present-day technologically sophisticated world really as marvellous and as miraculous as we seem to generally believe it is? 'Ah,' the philistines of materialist progress would retort to such a question, 'we are able to lead longer, happier, healthier and wealthier lives today due to modern technologies, economies, medicines, surgical techniques, and generally higher standards of living for a larger section of the population than in previous generations and in the non-Western world.' Ha! Ha! Do we indeed? Do people really live longer, happier and healthier lives today than in the past, or in non-Western cultures?

The natural, biological human life span has always stood around seventy years, 'three score years and ten', just as it did in Shakespeare's day, and as it stood in Biblical times, and as it stands today. In fact, in certain cases, our 'primitive' and less technologically sophisticated ancestors were noted for their extreme longevity. For example, Scottish Highlanders in the eighteenth century, the 'Wild Irish' (that is, 'uncivilised' and living outside the English 'Pale' of control) in the sixteenth century, English shepherds of the nineteenth century, Polynesian 'savages' before contact with Europeans, Ancient Greek sages, Native Americans, and religious ascetics not uncommonly lived to their eighties, nineties and even passed the century mark. As W.H. Hudson remarked,

'The memory of that vanished time, the thought that the ruder life of the past, when men lived nearer to Nature, had a keener flavour, is accompanied with a haunting regret. It is true that the regret is for something we have not known, that we have only heard or read of it, but it has become mixed in our mind with our very own experienced past – our glad beautiful 'days that are no more'…we may well believe that men were healthier and had better appetites than now – that they were all and always young.' (W.H. Hudson, *The Book of a Naturalist*).

It is a myth to suppose that people in the Ancient World or in 'primitive', less technologically sophisticated societies were, or are today, physically, mentally or spiritually inferior to the modern, civilised, Westerner in spite of our highly sophisticated medical and technological advancements. People in the Ancient World or in 'primitive' societies, without all of modern, Western man's miracles of science and technology, could and did survive to a ripe old age (and still do where such primitive societies have not been spoiled or corrupted by 'civilisation' and Western diseases). For example, King Ateas of the Scythians (wild, nomadic tribes of the Ukrainian steppes) was killed in battle near the Danube fighting against Philip the Second of Macedonia in 339 B.C., when he was ninety years of age. According to the author Josephus, in his book *The Jewish War* written in the first century A.D., the Essenes (a Jewish religious sect) were 'long-lived, *most of them* passing the century, owing to the simplicity of their daily life, I suppose, and the regular routine.' According to the Coffin Texts (Ancient Egyptian manuscripts) it is stated that 'He who understands life will live to a hundred and ten.' Famous Native American chiefs who survived to a ripe old age, in spite of the supposed 'primitive' lifestyle of the Indian 'savages', include Geronimo, who died in 1909 in his eightieth year; Red Cloud, who also died in 1909 in his eighty-seventh year; Catahecassa or Black Hoof, principal chief of the Shawnee, who died in 1831 in his ninety-first year; Kiontwogky or Cornplanter, a Seneca chief, who died in 1836 in his one hundred and first year; and Naw-Kaw, a Winnebago chief, who died in 1833 in his ninety-eighth year (Naw-Kaw was six feet tall, and when he met Thomas McKenney in Washington in 1828 at the age of ninety-three, he was still vigorous and muscular).

Famous Ancient Greek poets, sages and philosophers who lived to a ripe old age include Sophocles, who died in 406 B.C. in his eighty-ninth year; Plato, who died in 317 B.C. in his one hundred and tenth year; Thales of Miletus, who died in 546 B.C. in his ninety-fourth year; Timotheus of Miletus, who died in 357 B.C. in his ninetieth year; Accius, who died in 86 B.C. in his eighty-fourth year; Livius Andronicus, who died in 204 B.C. in his eightieth year; Pacuvius, who died in 130 B.C. in his ninetieth year; and Alexis, who died in 270 B.C. in his one hundred and second year. Even in the supposedly hard and brutal medieval period the natural, biological human lifespan still stood upwards of seventy years of age, barring disease, accident or violent death (which seems to have been quite prevalent in that war-like era, though was it more violent than the brutal twentieth century?). The natural, biological lifespan of people in the Middle Ages is shown in the following medieval manuscript from the twelfth century:

'The stages of man's life are six: Infancy, Boyhood, Adolescence, Manhood, Maturity and Old Age.

'The first is the age of childhood, of the little one growing towards the light of day, and this goes on for seven years. The second is boyhood, which is innocent, that is to say pure and not yet able to beget children, which continues until fourteen. The third, adolescence, is grown up enough to be a sire, and this stretches to twenty-eight. Manhood, the fourth, is the healthiest of all ages, finishing at fifty. The fifth state of the older man is maturity, which is a decline from youth into age, not yet old but no longer young...This age, beginning in the fiftieth year, is ended in the seventieth. The sixth period, or Old Age, is not bounded by any particular time in years. It extends, after the first five stages, so long as life remains, until it is ended by senectitude. Decline is the final stage of old age (senectutis) and is called so because it is the end of the sixth one (sextae aetatis). Into these six divisions have the philosophers parcelled out our human life, by which it changes and slips away and tends toward the conclusion of the grave.' (*The Book of Beasts*, a Latin bestiary of the twelfth century, edited by T.H. White)

It is both false and unjust for us arrogant, modern Westerners to denigrate the cultures or ways of life of our less technologically sophisticated, 'primitive' ancestors just because they lacked the technological and scientific inventions of present-day society. These inventions have not necessarily turned us into a kinder, a wiser, a more knowledgeable, a more spiritual, a more creative, a more aesthetically intelligent or even a more longer-lived creature, and we seem to be even less in tune with the living Earth and the Cosmos than we have ever been.

The Ancient Greeks and the Ancient Romans were a very learned, philosophical and knowledgeable people, no more ignorant or unenlightened or 'backward' intellectually than we are today. The Ancient Greeks, who passed onto the Romans their wide knowledge and learning, were aware of the existence of atoms (via the theories of Leucippus and Democritus of Abdera); were aware that the earth was round (via the theory of Pythagoras); were aware that the earth revolved around the sun in company with the other planets (via the theory of Aristarchus of Samos); had an accurate calculation of the circumference of the earth (by Eratosthenes and Dionysodorus); knew about evolution since Anaximander said that all living creatures arose from water, and that men had evolved from fish; knew that the earth was freely suspended in space (Anaximander); and were aware that human civilisation had an extremely long history (Epigenes, for example, believed that the Babylonians had kept astronomical observations inscribed on backed bricks which dated back for 730,000 years!) Yet, by the seventeenth century A.D., Archbishop James Ussher confidently calculated that the world had been created in just 4004 B.C.! The Ancient Greeks were even aware of the possible existence of a huge, undiscovered continent, that is, the Americas, between Europe and eastern Asia. Plato states in his book *Timaeus* that there is a 'passage west from Atlantis [the mythical island] to the rest of the islands [the West Indies?], as well as from these islands to the *whole opposite continent that surrounds the real sea*' [the Atlantic Ocean(?) which is a real sea, unlike the Mediterranean Sea, which is a land-locked body of water, and the Americas do indeed 'surround' the Atlantic in a half circle north to south].

Knowledge and learning were never entirely extinguished in Europe, even after the fall of Rome (to both 'barbarians' and to fanatical Christians), and the subsequent 'Dark' Ages and the medieval period. The Moors and Arabs of Spain/North Africa, together with a few monks and scholars in Europe (especially in Ireland), kept safe and indeed developed the knowledge of the Ancient World, until it was reborn to a wider audience in the Renaissance. Learned people in Europe in the Middle Ages did not believe that the earth was flat, as is commonly supposed, since they were well aware of the theories of the Ancient Greeks, which they studied and debated in secret. This is explained by the author Hendrik Van Loon in his *History of Man*:

'During the last two hundred years of the Roman Empire the thinking part of the population had accepted this hypothesis [a spherical earth revolving around the sun with a number of other planets] as something so self-evident that it could no longer be considered a subject for debate. But when the Church became all-powerful, in the fifth century, it was no longer safe to harbour such ideas, least of all that one which proclaimed the earth to be round. We should not judge them too harshly. In the first place, the earliest converts to Christianity generally belonged to those classes of society that had been the least exposed to the current learning of the times. And, furthermore, they were firmly convinced that the end of the world was near at hand, when Christ would return to the former scene of His sufferings to separate the good from the evil. He would return in the midst of all His glory and for everyone to behold. But, so they reasoned, and quite correctly from their own point of view, if this were to be the case (and they had no doubt upon the subject) then the world must be flat. For otherwise Christ would have to make His appearance twice – one for the benefit of the people on the western hemisphere and once for the benefit of those on the other side of the world. Such a procedure, of course, would be absurd and undignified, and therefore entirely out of the question.

'The Church, therefore, for almost a thousand years insisted upon teaching that the earth was a flat disc and that it was the centre of the universe. In learned circles, among the scientists of a few of the monasteries and among the astronomers of some of the rapidly growing cities, the old Greek conception of a round world, revolving around the sun, together with a number of other planets, was never quite discarded. Most of the men who held this to be true did not openly dare to talk about the subject, but kept their ideas strictly to themselves. For they knew that a public discussion would merely upset the peace and quiet of millions of their less intelligent fellow-citizens while it would do nothing to bring the solution of the problem any nearer.

'Since then, the Church people too, with very few exceptions, have been forced to accept the notion that the planet on which we live must be a ball. By the end of the fifteenth century the evidence in favour of this ancient Greek theory had become too overwhelming to be refuted any longer...'

Learned people in Europe in the Middle Ages could be just as intelligent and as intellectually curious as learned people in the world today, such as, for example, Gerald of Wales (Giraldus Cambrensis), a Norman-Welsh author who lived from 1145 to 1223 (he lived to the ripe old age of seventy-eight!). His description of the writer's/storyteller's craft, and his obviously wide reading of the ancient classics, show that medieval people were not all stupid, illiterate, ignorant, ill-educated and unenlightened (which seems to be the modern view-point, and reading the following passage written by Gerald of Wales it makes you wonder who really is the less enlightened, them or us?):

'As far as I am concerned, ever since I was a boy, I have been inspired by a love of literature, and the art of writing has had a peculiar attraction for me. I have always had a great thirst for knowledge, and I have pursued my researches into the works of nature farther than most of my contemporaries. For the benefit of those who will come after, I have also rescued from oblivion some of the remarkable events of our own times. This cannot be achieved without great labour, but I have enjoyed doing it. The research-work necessary if one is to find out just what really happened is not at all easy. Even when one has discovered the truth in all its detail, there still remains the task of ordering one's facts, and this is difficult, too. To maintain a correct balance from beginning to end, and, indeed, throughout the whole course of one's narrative, and to exclude all irrelevant material, is not easy. Then there is the problem of the choice of words and expressions, and of how to perfect one's style, if one wants to write well. It is one thing to set out the course of events in proper sequence, but you still have the difficult problem of deciding what words to use and how best to express what you want to say. Writing is an exacting business. First you decide what to leave out, and then you have to polish up what you put in. What you finally commit to parchment must face the eagle eye of many readers, now and in the future, and at the same time run the risk of meeting hostile criticism. The words one speaks fly off on the wind and are heard no more: you can praise or condemn, but it is soon forgotten. What you write down and then give to the world in published form is never lost: it lasts forever, to the glory or ignominy of him who wrote it. As Seneca says: "The critical reader mulls over what is said well and what is ill-expressed, enjoying them both, for he is looking for faults. He wants to find good things which he can praise, but he is only too ready to laugh at anything ridiculous." To this the poet adds: "He picks on what is bad, is prompt to sneer, And soon forgets the good he should revere." Among the pursuits which we should most admire, there are other things to be said in favour of the studious life. "History," says Seneca again, "is the recording of past events, the testimony of the ages, the light of truth, a living memory, a guide for conduct and a reminder of what happened long ago." I find this sort of work the more attractive in that it seems to me to be more praiseworthy to write something worth quoting oneself than simply to keep on quoting other people, and better to be admired by others for one's own compositions than to be a sound critic of what others have composed. It is good to praise others, but it is better to be praised by them. I am strengthened and encouraged by these pleasing thoughts: I would rather be like Jerome than Croesus; to riches themselves I prefer the man who scorns them. This, then, is my joy and my delight. My modest way of life suits me better than any rich living could do; I prefer my honest poverty to affluence which I do not want. What one owns must always perish, but what I have will live. Possessions pass away, but my skills live forever. Fame I prefer to money, I would rather have glory than wealth.'

Chapter Forty-Three

Depletion of Nature

How astonishing it would be if we were able to return to the past and visit old England, today one of the most highly populated, intensively managed, agriculturally cultivated and tamed lands in Europe, as it once was before the Enclosure Acts and the Industrial Revolution. How amazed we would be to see the abundance of nature back then, before intensive farming practices, urbanisation, massive road construction, extensive quarrying, mining, and game-keeping, entirely wiped out, or reduced in range or abundance, so much of England's heritage of wildlife. Where in today's England are the glorious and noble birds of prey, except the common little kestrel, compared to the numbers and variety there once were, until the early nineteenth century, before the enclosures of the commons and Victorian game-keeping destroyed our raptors and eagles (to produce pheasants and evict peasants, as well as the local wildlife for the privileged elite!). However, in recent years there has been a remarkable comeback for some of our English birds of prey, such as the red kite (from its stronghold in Wales), and long may this trend continue!

And if we were to travel further back in time still, to the Early Middle Ages, even wolves were abundant in England, and beavers were still to be found living wild on the River Teifi in Wales (as described at the time by the author Gerald of Wales). Where are the large carnivorous and herbivorous mammals in England, which are still to be found in other parts of Europe, such as the wolf, the brown bear, the wild boar, the beaver, the aurochs or wild ox (this species is now entirely extinct in the wild, except for a few cattle in zoos or parks which resemble the aurochs, and have been selectively bred from domesticated cattle who are descended from the wild ox), the reindeer, the elk, and the lynx? Alas! They are no longer resident as wild animals in England, since they were either hunted to extinction long ago, or their habitats were destroyed mainly at the hands of man (though changes in climate may also have played a part, as in the extinction of the reindeer).

Consider Hereward the Wake, the Anglo-Saxon hero, who found refuge from the Norman conquerors of England in the vast wilderness of the Fens of East Anglia one thousand years ago. The Fenland in those days was a vast pathless wilderness of rushy swamps, scrubby islets, and open meres, which provided refuge for huge flocks of birds, including pelicans, herons, white storks, cranes, white spoonbills, bitterns, avocets, ruffs, curlews, godwits, all types of wild ducks, buzzards, kites, marsh harriers, ospreys, and so forth. Today the Fenland is a vast, flat, monotonous 'green desert' of arable fields, farms, roads and drainage canals, and only a tiny fraction of the original marshland is left ('all are appropriate, bog, and marsh, and fen, are only poor to undiscerning men', to quote the poet George Crabbe). And what happened to the people the Fens provided a living for – the fishermen, the reed-cutters, the hunters for sport or for food? What about their needs, as well as the needs of the wildlife? The Fens were drained to provide food for the populations of the vastly expanding cities of England between the seventeenth and late nineteenth centuries.

How utterly barren, tame and devoid of life the much beloved English countryside would appear to an Anglo-Saxon lord, or a medieval baron, if he were to return today somehow and visit his ancient hunting-grounds, as the native forests have been almost all felled, the marshes almost all drained, the common lands enclosed, the big or fierce animals exterminated, the great birds of prey driven off to the remotest cliffs and mountain ranges, and wild, uncultivated nature subjugated in our over-populated and intensively managed English landscape. The writer G.M. Trevelyan describes how wild and primitive England must once have been in Anglo-Saxon times, 'What a place it must have been, that virgin woodland wilderness of old England, ever encroached on by innumerable peasant clearings, but still harbouring God's plenty of all manner of beautiful birds and beasts, and still rioting in a vast wealth of trees and flowers…In certain respects the conditions of pioneer life in the Shires of Saxon England and the Danelaw were not unlike those of North America and Australia in the nineteenth-century – the lumberman with his axe, the log shanty in the clearing, the draught oxen, the horses to ride to the nearest farm five miles away across the wilderness, the weapon ever laid close to hand beside the axe and the plough, the rough word and ready blow, and the good comradeship of the frontiersman...Every one of the sleepy, leisurely garden-like villages of rural England (today) was once a pioneer settlement, an outpost of man planted and battled for in the midst of nature's primaeval realm.' Although this description is a slight exaggeration (England had been settled by farming peoples for thousands of years before the Anglo-Saxons arrived, so it was hardly all a pioneer wilderness), it is somewhat true, since both the Romans and the Celts avoided the low-lying, clayey forests, since they harboured malaria (ague) and they had not the axes to cut down the heavy oaks and hornbeams. They mainly settled on the chalky downlands of southern England, with a lighter covering of beeches and on which they could graze their animals, when the forests on the downs had been felled and the grasslands converted to pasture.

Other countries, too, such as Israel, although still rich in wildlife (there are seventy surviving species of mammal in Israel), had an even richer fauna in Biblical times. Although Israel still has wild animals such as the gazelle, wild boar, ibex, hyena, wolf, jackal, Syrian hyrax, caracal, lynx, and leopard (rediscovered in the 1970s), it had a much richer and even more exotic fauna in Biblical times (and right up until the nineteenth century!). This fauna included the roe deer, fallow deer, addax, European bison, oryx, wild goat, wild ox, lion, Syrian bear, cheetah, hippopotamus, water buffalo, Syrian and Arabian wild onager (wild ass or wild donkey of the Bible?), wild sheep, wild camel (?), crocodile, and ostrich. These animals are now all extinct in Israel, primarily due to man's hunting activities and through the destruction of natural habitats. Yet without these animals in the wild in Israel how can the world be a richer place today than in the past? How has humankind 'progressed' if the fauna and flora, God's Creations, of Israel have been depleted or destroyed?

Chapter Forty-Four

Immortal Flowers

The future prospects for the survival of wild nature in the highly populated, industrialised/industrialising, developed/developing world today could be viewed both pessimistically and optimistically. There has probably never been such a widespread awareness about the harm humankind is doing to the natural world, yet, at the same time, carelessness, cynicism, and the misuse of modern technologies and sciences have never had such a capacity to destroy the living earth, seas, and airs, for humankind's short term, self-seeking, purely materialistic needs.

Surely we ought to try our utmost to preserve and conserve what remains of wild nature on this earth, when one considers the natural wealth and abundance we have destroyed in the past, how we have exterminated, depleted or driven out so many species of wild plant and wild animal, and the natural habitats we have removed for cities and farmlands, or simply polluted with our waste and chemical poisons. Our miraculous sciences and technologies should be utilised not to destroy but to conserve, to re-create, to re-habilitate, and to restore at least some of the natural world we have destroyed in our rush for 'progress'. Humankind needs more than ever to escape from the stresses and the artificiality of modern life.

The time and energy we spend on trying to amass for ourselves wealth and perishable personal possessions, or on trying to produce an over-abundance of cash crops, rather than foodstuffs we need to eat, or on building road networks, which not only destroy landscapes but lead to ever more pollution and stress levels. We should be trying to preserve and conserve the remaining bits of wild nature which still survive, instead of obliterating them in the pursuit of our false utopian dream of speed, efficiency, economic competition, materialism, and technological progress, since such a 'progress' often displays little responsibility to future generations or to the world itself, our home.

We cannot afford to lose a single species of plant or animal unnecessarily since, '…like immortal flowers they have drifted down to us on the ocean of time, and their strangeness and beauty bring to our imaginations a dream and a picture of that unknown world, immeasurably far removed, where man was not: and when they perish, something of gladness goes out from nature, and the sunshine loses something of its brightness…They are links in a chain, and branches on the tree of life, with their roots in a past inconceivably remote, and but for our action they would continue to flourish…' (W.H. Hudson, *The Naturalist in La Plata*)

Modern, Western, affluent, acquisitive, technologically-fixated, materialistic, scientifically reductionist, economically competitive, and self-seeking humankind is not of itself the highest or the best creature the world has ever experienced, or even the most truly intelligent. Do people today really have a higher aesthetic intelligence than previous generations, or a deeper attachment to the natural rhythms of the world and the universe, or, are we actually more conformist to artificial, bourgeois, material values, more greedy-minded, more self-seeking, more homogenised, less culturally diverse, and lacking the crafts and artistic skills of humankind even in the Middle Ages (with all of our mass produced, pre-fabricated, machine-made products and buildings)? Where can one find today the pomp, ceremony, sumptuous costumes, splendour and magnificence of the Middle Ages (except in a few surviving festivals and processions). The Middle Ages was an era of awe-inspiring cathedrals, gorgeous pageants, religious processions, beautiful costumes, and people of all classes indulged and inspired themselves with these things, even the poorest peasants had a rich religious life and wore graceful costumes on holidays (looking at paintings in illuminated manuscripts depicting medieval peasants working in the fields, even their shabbiest working costumes were more graceful then the business-uniforms of today). Yet the Middle Ages are seen today as backward, primitive, coarse and brutal. And what about the supposedly 'savage' and 'heathen' Aztecs of old Mexico, with their massive temples, their huge aviaries of beautiful humming birds and parrots, and the feather embroidery or feather tapestry they once delighted in, and with which they could produce all the effects of delicate pictures (a craft and art now sadly lost to the world)? Are we moderns really more 'advanced' than these 'primitive' and 'backward' peoples or cultures, or are we simply puffed up with our own conceit and inflated egos, lost to materialism and utilitarianism?

If only as temporary escape from the stress, pollution, confinement, and hustle-and-bustle of modern life in cities, towns, suburbs and houses; or to re-awaken one's sense of the beauty and wonder of life in all of its abundance and diversity of forms; or to remember our connection to the living Earth; or for poetic, intellectual, spiritual, and artistic inspiration; or purely for health and recreation, then large areas of this world (since there is still room enough for nature, as well as development, if we are wise and careful enough) must be set inalienably aside for wild, uncultivated nature. Even if we never manage to visit all these places, just the thought that Nature, and unspoilt wildernesses, still exist on this increasingly 'getting and spending' earth, is enough: a dream, a vision and indeed a reality of untainted, spontaneous, abundant beauty and life, sorely needed in the current times.

In the Jewish tradition it is believed that people once lived in harmony with the animals before the Fall and even understood their language, and according to the prophet Isaiah, when the Messianic Kingdom is proclaimed humankind, the wild beasts and all the creatures will be reconciled. But can we wait until that day, since if humankind continues to 'develop' wild nature off the face of the earth, and to wastefully consume the earth's finite natural resources, we will have few wild creatures left to share our planet with, or rather, can we begin the reconciliation and repairing between humankind and nature now?

Chapter Forty-Five

The Perfection of Humankind

Many so-called 'primitive', 'backward', 'savage', or 'heathen' cultures across the world prior to their conquest and colonisation by the European powers (and this colonisation was not to bring peace and prosperity to the 'benighted natives', but in order to impose Western goods, ideas, religions and will on the native inhabitants), had a wise and enlightened understanding of the forces and balance of nature, as well as their own sophisticated bodies of knowledge in the arts and the sciences. In the process of conquest and colonisation, with its attendant loss of life and destruction, much of the knowledge and learning of the defeated natives was deliberately or unwittingly obliterated. The native inhabitants were not necessarily defeated by the Western powers because they were more 'primitive' or 'backward' (mentally, culturally, spiritually, physically, intellectually, socially, or morally) than the Europeans, but because the European powers had better weapons and killing machines, not to mention the introduction, accidental or not, of new and deadly diseases hitherto unknown in the newly colonised lands, as well as the poison of alcohol to peoples unused to such a potent concoction.

The Native North American Indians, for example, however technologically simple and unsophisticated in the eyes of the European invaders (considering the comparative sophistication of European science and industry), had a way of life uncorrupted by the Western world's life-withering, hierarchical, dogmatic, exploitative and selfish ideologies, whether political, religious or scientific. The native peoples of North and South America were not defeated by a superior or a more advanced culture, but by the European invaders' superior firepower, his greater numbers, his deadly infectious diseases, his alcohol, his devious commerce, and his constraining religions. However, one should not over-romanticise the Native Americans (since they practised war, infanticide, torture of captured enemies, and slavery) or over-demonise the European settlers, since there has probably never existed on the earth a perfect, utopian society. However, the Native American inhabitants did possess many admirable and enlightened ideas more in tune with the Cosmos and much more 'earth-centred' than the religions of the Europeans.

There is to found amongst the teachings and traditions of Native Americans the concept or understanding that humankind is but a part of nature, a small but integral part of a greater whole, a strand in the web of life, and not so arrogant as to think, which many Western religions and modern science today, believe, that man is the 'Lord of Creation', a Creation or natural world that needs be conquered, controlled, manipulated, exploited and transformed by art or science for purely selfish and materialistic ends, and not for the entire community. Many Western religions lack any reverence or respect for nature and the natural world, or ignore it completely (though there are of course exceptions to this, such as the teachings of Saint Francis of Assisi in the Roman Catholic religion, or Hassidic teachings in the Jewish faith, or Sufism in the Islamic tradition).

Traditional Native American beliefs point out that nature is alive and conscious, even the rocks and stones as well as the very earth itself, that we live in a living universe, a great living web of Creation, in which humankind is a thread. They believe that humankind should try to live in tune with the Cosmos, and not puffed up with such egotistical conceit as to believe we can master or separate ourselves from the world, physically or intellectually, or that we are somehow 'Lords' over it. In the words of the great Anglo-Argentine author W.H. Hudson, who grew up in Argentina in the nineteenth century before its spoilation by the European colonisers, the ancient, mystical faculty, such as that possessed by the Native American or by anyone who has retained something of the child in him or herself, is '...a sense of the supernatural in all natural things. We may say, in fact, that unless the soul goes out to meet what we see we do not see it; nothing do we see, not a beetle, not a blade of grass.' (*The Book of a Naturalist*)

The nineteenth-century Native American Indian prophet and dreamer Smohalla (of the Northwest American Indian Wanapum tribe) spoke out against any interference with the earth, and advocated strict adherence to Indian values and modes of life. He was actively opposed to white American ways of living, and stated,

'My young men shall never work. Men who work cannot dream; and wisdom comes to us in dreams.

You ask me to plough the ground! Shall I take a knife and tear my mother's breast? Then when I die she will not take me to her bosom to rest.

You ask me to dig for stone! Shall I dig under her skin for her bones? Then when I die I cannot enter her body to be born again.

You ask me to cut grass and make hay and sell it and be rich like white men! But how dare I cut off my mother's hair?'

Sitting Bull was not impressed by the white man's way of life and preferred the Indian way. He said, 'The life my people want is a life of freedom. I have seen nothing that a white man has, houses or railways or clothing or food, that is as good as the right to move in the open country, and live in our fashion.'

Chief Seattle also spoke in defence of Indian ways and values in 1854, and an earth-centred philosophy of life, 'We are part of the Earth and the Earth is part of us. The fragrant flowers are our sisters. The reindeer, the horse, the great eagle are our brothers. The rocky heights, the foamy crests of waves in the rivers, the sap of meadow flowers, the body heat of the pony – and of human beings – all belong to the same family... Humankind has not woven the web of life. We are but one thread within it. Whatever we do to the web, we do to ourselves. All things are bound together. All things connect. Whatever befalls the Earth befalls also the children of the Earth.'

Although many Native American societies were fairly primitive or unsophisticated in comparison with contemporaneous European advances in science and industry (although the Aztecs and Incas equalled or even surpassed Europeans in many arts and sciences, before their conquest), they had a quite highly developed and intellectual body of beliefs, and a system which was certainly less obsessed than in the West with personal possessions (which were given to other members of the tribe in 'give away ceremonies' which actually enhanced the donator's prestige), private property (land was held communally), religious hierarchy and selfish individualism.

The extermination of the bison, once sixty million strong on the prairies of the American West, was seen as a positive achievement by some 'civilised' Americans, such as General Sheridan, along with the extermination of the native Indians, who depended on the bison for their physical survival. General Sheridan said, 'It is a sentimental error to legislate in favour of the bison. You should, on the contrary, congratulate the skin hunters and give each of them a bronze medal with on one side the image of a dead bison and on the other that of a distressed Indian. The hide hunters have done more to solve the Indian problem than the whole of the American Army in thirty years. The extermination of the bison is the only way of founding a lasting peace and of favouring the progress of civilisation.' So, in other words, General Sheridan is saying that 'progress' and 'civilisation' in the United States is founded on the destruction and exploitation of nature and finite natural resources, as well as the oppression and pauperisation, even deliberate extinction, of the indigenous inhabitants of America. But, one asks, how can a 'lasting peace' and a truly civilised society come forth from destruction, exploitation, pauperisation, oppression and extermination?

The buffalo hunter Frank H. Mayer admitted it was sheer greed and U.S. government policy (which favoured extermination of the bison as a way to wipe out the Indians), that were the primary reasons for the ruthless destruction of the vast buffalo herds. He said, 'Maybe we runners [buffalo hunters] served our purpose in helping abolish the buffalo; maybe it was our ruthless harvesting of him which telescoped the control of the Indian by a decade or maybe more. Or maybe I am just rationalising. Maybe we were just a greedy lot who wanted to get ours, and to hell with posterity, the buffalo, or anyone else, just so we kept our scalps on and our money pouches filled. I think maybe that is the way it was.' (Ward, *The West: An Illustrated History*)

The commander at Fort Dodge described the slaughter of the buffalo herds and all the other game of the prairies in shocking vividness: 'Where there were myriads of buffalo the year before there were now myriads of carcasses. The air was foul with a sickening stench, and the vast plain, which only a short twelvemonth before teemed with animal life, was a dead, solitary, putrid desert.' (Ward, *The West: An Illustrated History*)

Some white Americans did recognise the Red Man's qualities, such as the author and painter George Catlin who became obsessed by the vanishing Indian in the nineteenth century. He fulfilled his life's desire by painting a record of the costumes and ceremonies of practically every surviving Indian tribe in the United States of America, and when he had done this he travelled to South America to record the life and character of the native Indian tribes there. According to George Catlin the 'Red Man' was 'a truly lofty and noble race', 'honourable and highly intellectual' (yet other white observers of the time called the Native Americans 'ignorant savages'), 'honest, hospitable, faithful, brave, warlike, cruel, revengeful, relentless, yet honourable, contemplative and religious' (which seems like a much more rounded portrayal of a people than the over-romanticisms or, on the other hand, the cruel stereotypes of Hollywood).

Other more selfish or grasping white Americans were not so impressed by the Red Man. When Senator Henry Dawes (b.1816-d.1903) of Massachusetts described the Cherokee's tribal and communal way of life he thought that 'the defect of the system was apparent. They have got as far as they can go, because they hold their land in common…There is no selfishness, which is at the bottom of civilisation.' The American Indian's generosity and lack of selfishness proved to be his undoing, and why his way of life could not be tolerated in America's greedy and venal civilisation. In 1851 the Secretary of the Interior put it bluntly: 'To tame the savage you must tie him down to the soil. You must make him understand the value of property, and the benefits of its separate ownership. You must appeal to those selfish principles implanted by divine providence in the nature of man for the wisest purposes.' George Catlin did not agree with this corrupt philosophy, and described his admiration for the Indian's honesty and selflessness, 'I love a people who have always made me welcome to the best they had, who are honest without laws, who have no jails and no poorhouse, who worship God without a Bible – and I believe that God loves them also – who have never raised a hand against me, or stolen my property, where there was no law to punish either, and oh! How I love a people who don't live for the love of money!'

In 1562, several American Indians were brought to France, and when they were asked what they thought about Parisian culture and society, they replied that they were not so very much impressed. As related by the French writer and philosopher Montaigne the Indians could not understand how '…some men [were] gorged to the full with things of every sort, while their other halves were beggars at their doors, emaciated with hunger and poverty. They found it strange that the poverty-stricken half should suffer such injustice, and that they did not take the others by the throat or set fire to their houses.' This 'poverty-stricken half' did exactly that two centuries later in the French Revolution of 1789! And the 'poverty-stricken half' also rebelled against injustice, set fire to houses and took 'the others by the throat' in the Russian Revolution and Civil War from 1917 to 1922, and in the Irish War of Independence and Civil War from 1916 to 1922, whether for good or for ill.

For all of the much boasted achievements of Western civilisation, in science, industry, democracy, technology, etc. are we really so enlightened when we compare ourselves to so-called 'primitive' cultures? If, as Rousseau suggested two and a half centuries ago, 'civilised' European society really was so much better and happier than 'savage' societies, then how was it that the 'poor' savages, '...consistently refuse to govern themselves in imitation of us or learn to live happily among us, whereas one reads in a thousand places that Frenchmen and other Europeans have voluntarily taken refuge among these peoples, spent their whole lives there without being able to quit such a strange way of life, and we see sensible missionaries tenderly lamenting calm and innocent days spent among these much despised peoples?' (J.J. Rousseau, *Discourse on the Origin and Foundations of Inequality among Men*). Rousseau adds that 'Nothing can overcome the savages' unconquerable revulsion at the prospect of embracing our morals and style of life.' Yet American 'Indian policy' was seen in the nineteenth century as a 'civilising mission'. Indian commissioner T.J. Morgan believed that 'The Indians must conform to "the white man's ways", peaceably if they will, forcibly if they must. The tribal relations should be broken up, *socialism destroyed* and the family and the autonomy of the individual substituted.' Another Indian commissioner Oberly believed that, with the breaking up of Indian tribal lands into individual allotments, the Indians would then be able to emulate 'the *exalting egotism* of American civilization, so that he [the Indian] will say "I" instead of "We", and "This is mine", instead of "This is ours".' The assault on Indian tribal land ownership was passed into legislation in 1887 with the Dawes General Allotment Act. The Americans '...called their conquest, their driving to starvation, of the indigenous Red Indians in order to provide homes for right-thinking homesteaders, "Manifest Destiny".' (Glynn, *Skin To Skin: Eroticism in Dress*)

Most Western states have been ceaselessly embroiled in destructive wars, ethnic, political, religious, or economic, since time immemorial, whether or not we like to view ourselves as 'civilised' and 'highly developed' nations. In fact, the more 'developed' and 'civilised' we become the more destructive and deadly we seem to behave, since advancements in technology generally lead to advancements in the art and science of warfare, killing techniques and mass destruction, and our economic systems become more able and efficient to support the war machine. We still seem to be fighting the same old ethnic conflicts that we were embroiled in hundreds or even thousands of years ago in order to possess the same tiny portion of the earth, and the only difference being a greater capacity for mass destruction of life, property and the environment. Jews and Palestinians in the 'Holy Land' (so-called!), just like sectarian factions in Northern Ireland, are still fighting the same old battles and senselessly killing the 'enemy' as they were hundreds or thousands of years ago. One has only to read Josephus' 'The Jewish War' written two thousand years ago with its descriptions of Arabs fighting Hebrews for control of Palestine, or read the old Irish epics dating back to pre-Christian Ireland with descriptions of tribal battles in Northern Ireland, to realise we have not really become more civilised, in spite of all our wonderful technology, and we can now lay mines, plant bombs, shoot each other from long distances, rain down destruction from the sky, etc. Yet we see ourselves as more advanced and enlightened!

Though the Western world conquered and colonised the world through its industrial, technological and military might, it was really no more noble or better or wiser than the vanquished native peoples, and maybe the very triumph of the West proves it is the most aggressive, savage, devious, or manipulative force on the face of the earth. Else how could it have conquered the world? Even the Western world's dominant religion – Christianity – is very often in practice not the way of life as espoused by Christ himself. Organised Christian religion allied to political power structures has often proved to be a narrow-minded, intellectually conformist, oppressive, repressive and destructive philosophy in the world at large. Christianity in practice has often led to superstition, subservience, the elimination of intellectual freedom, and finally mass emigration or mass expulsion – as occurred in the most pious of Catholic Christian countries, namely Holy Catholic Spain, which could not tolerate any questioning of orthodox Catholic beliefs by its adherents, or tolerate any other religions practising in its territories. Catholic monarchs and priests killed or expulsed all the Protestants, Jews and Muslims from Spain. However, on the other hand, the Catholic Church did provide sponsorship for the arts which led to the construction of magnificent cathedrals and sublime works of art, by such masters as Michelangelo, Raphael, Leonardo da Vinci, Benvenuto Cellini, etc. etc. The Church also provided welfare for the poor and spiritual comfort.

However, the history of fanatical Christian intolerance cannot be whitewashed.[8] Brutal Spanish conquistadors (in the name of the Spanish Crown) aided and abetted by fanatical Catholic priests (in the name of Christ), deliberately destroyed not only the lives and liberty of the defeated Aztecs, Incas and other native peoples in Central and South America, but also their highly sophisticated astronomical and historical records, in order to obliterate the culture of those peoples, and force them into subservience to the Spanish Crown and the Catholic fold.[9]

Christian Crusaders, who were fighting to take control of the Holy Land from the Saracens in the Middle Ages, mercilessly butchered not only the Muslim Saracens, but also the native Christian Copts, Armenians, Jews, Byzantine and Greek Orthodox Christians in the name of Christ and the Holy Mother Church.

The Moors of southern Spain, a highly cultured and learned people, and who had quite a religiously tolerant society (except under Berber rule for short periods[10]), were cruelly and treacherously expelled from Spain, along with the Jewish population, after the Christian Reconquista (Reconquest) in 1492.

The enmity towards, and intolerance of, non-Christian cultures and beliefs by the Spanish and Portuguese Catholic Empires in South and Central America (as well as by Puritan emigrants in North America, it must be added), led to perhaps the most cruel acts of

---

[8] It must be added here that organised pagan religions could be as intolerant and as cruel as organised Christianity, including the burning of Christians in Ancient Rome under Nero, the persecution of Jews by the Roman Emperors in Palestine, and forcing all the citizens of the Roman Empire, whatever their faith, to worship the Roman Emperor as a living god, rather than just the powerful leader he was, as Jews and Christians maintained.

[9] The Aztecs had highly developed systems of astronomy, mathematics, architectural methods, calendars, and even indoor plumbing, which were almost all obliterated during the conquest and 'pacification' of the Aztec Empire by the conquistadors.

[10] The Moors generally tolerated, and even welcomed, Jews and Christians in their territories. Only under the Almoravides and even more fanatical Almohades were Christians and Jews persecuted. The Almoravides and Almohades were Muslim Berber tribes who ruled Moorish Spain for brief periods. They were generally less tolerant of 'unbelievers'.

plunder, violence, fraud and exploitation the world has ever witnessed, since the Native Americans were seen as even worse 'sinners' than the Muslims or Jews of Europe, because they were not merely seen as heretics or infidels, but as heathens, devil worshippers and pagans.

The accusation of heathenism, paganism and devil worship was extended to include so-called witches or sorcerers by the Inquisition. Between the thirteenth and eighteenth centuries Christian zealots (of both the Catholic and Puritan faiths), that is, priests, inquisitors and so-called 'witch-finders' (such as the notorious Matthew Hopkins), killed, persecuted and oppressed anybody who they deemed to have strayed from the 'orthodox' Christian faith, including so called heretics, blasphemers, apostates, and 'witches'. Yet many of these so called 'witches'[11] were simply rural folk healers, midwives and herbalists, who possessed certain powers or knowledge, which the hierarchical religious orthodoxy could not tolerate. No less than 40,000 (some sources put the estimate between 250,000 and one million) 'witches' or 'sorcerers' were killed between the early fifteenth century and the eighteenth century, when the killing or persecuting of so-called 'witches' became unacceptable in European society at large. The Spanish Inquisition was the most far-reaching. It commenced in 1478 and was officially abolished in 1834. It covered all of Spain and its foreign dominions. It claimed perhaps up to 375,000 lives, including heretics, 'witches', 'sorcerers', crypto-Muslims ('moriscos'), and crypto-Jews ('marranos' or 'conversos'). Moriscos and marranos were Jews or Muslims who had converted to Catholicism for convenience, but who still allegedly practised their faiths in secret.

One of the most tragic and disgraceful crimes which intolerant Christian fanatics ever perpetrated was setting fire to the library at Alexandria, which was the greatest repository of knowledge and wisdom in the Ancient World. This library is said to have contained over 700,000 works. The library was set alight by a mob of Christian fanatics, since it contained pagan works out of line with orthodox Christian thought, and the library's female curator was flayed alive

---

[11] The word 'witch' comes from 'watch' or 'wise women', that is, women who 'kept the watch'. Keeping the watch referred to lunar observations useful for agriculture and midwifery. However, these lunar observations were not in keeping with the Catholic and Puritan Churches, or rather, out of the political, economic and social control of them. Therefore, Witch Hunting and the Holy Inquisition were instigated.

with scallop shells. Yet we blame the heathen barbarians for destroying the knowledge and wisdom of the Ancient World (such as when they sacked Rome) but Christian fanaticism destroyed far more.

The brilliant fifteenth century astronomer Copernicus was forced to recant his scientific discovery that the earth revolved around the sun with the other planets, simply because it was incompatible with the Church's erroneous belief in a universe with the earth at its centre. Yet most literate people in the West, since at least the days of Ancient Greece, would have been aware of theories, such as that of Aristarchus of Samos, which investigated whether the earth revolved around the sun, and whether it was spherical and revolved on its axis. Yet the Church, in spite of all the evidence and simply to fit in with various orthodox Christian beliefs, still insisted the earth was flat and was situated in the centre of the universe. Much of the knowledge of Ancient Greece, Rome and Egypt only survived because the Muslim Arabs and Moors, less fanatical than the early Christians, preserved all the surviving Greek and Roman classics, and later passed them onto the less literate European lands, hungry for knowledge.

The slaughter, enslavement, physical and cultural genocide of indigenous peoples by the European powers during colonisation is a tragic and shocking history. In only one century (from 1519 to 1619) following the Spanish conquest of the Aztecs, the native population of Mexico fell from about 25 million persons to just 1.5 million. The native population of the Americas, north and south, has been estimated at about 70 or 80 million persons in 1492 (just prior to Columbus' landing), yet only three centuries later, in 1792, the native population had fallen to just 7 or 10 million persons. New diseases from Europe, famines, massacres, slavery, suicide or just sheer despair wiped out almost ninety or even ninety-five per cent of the native population of the Americas, probably the greatest genocide and most tragic clash of cultures in world history. Even contemporary Spaniards were shocked at the cruelty, brutality and violence of the Spanish and other European colonisers towards the native Indians in the Americas. Jose de Acosta confesses, 'We have exploited and plundered these poor people to such an extent that it seems the Europeans are more anxious to decide who has the right to plunder them, rather than make any attempt to protect their human rights. We have not given them Christianity and sincerity but under compulsion, fraud and violence. Never has such cruelty been seen in history in any invasion – by

Greeks or barbarians.' (Wood, *Legacy: A Search for the Origins of Civilisation*)

The indigenous people of the Caribbean (the Taino or Arawak), became extinct within fifty years of Columbus' landing, as a direct result of Spanish violence, forced labour and diseases. Columbus described the Taino/Arawak as '…in all the world no better people.' Unlike the war-like Carib Indians who practised ritual cannibalism and had invaded the Caribbean shortly before Columbus' arrival, the Taino/Arawak hardly ever went to war among each other, and even violence was rare. There were even female chiefs (caciques) among them. Apart from present-day descendants of the Taino/Arawak of very mixed blood in the Caribbean (of mixed Spanish, black and Indian extraction), and some written descriptions by European settlers, the only survival of the Taino/Arawak society are a few words in modern Spanish and English, such as hamaca (hammock), huracan (hurricane), and barbacoa (barbecue).

At least 15 million native Africans were annihilated as a result of slave-trading activities between the sixteenth and nineteenth centuries. Slave trading was carried out by the Arabs, the European powers, and by some West African leaders themselves, who sold African slaves to the white and Arab slavers.

It took just seventy years for Spanish colonisers to annihilate the native people of the Canary Islands (Europe's last Neolithic culture) during the sixteenth century, and the same time (seventy years) for European colonisers to wipe out the native inhabitants of Tasmania during the nineteenth century.

According to George Catlin, the native population of North America totalled about sixteen million persons prior to the arrival of the first European colonisers. By the 1830s the native population had fallen to just two million persons (by 1900 it was less than a million), and this loss of life, according to George Catlin, was the direct result '…of the small-pox, the sword, the bayonet, and whiskey…' of the White Man.

This terrible loss of life suffered by the indigenous peoples of the world, as a result of conquest and colonisation by the Western powers, is not to deny or detract from the delights, material comforts, wonders and miracles (scientific, technological, industrial) which the Western powers have developed, but merely to shed some light on the victims of Western imperialism, a considerable number of casualties whose bones and wrecked civilisations lie beneath the European coloniser's cities, schools, factories and farmlands to this very day, especially in the Americas.

The lie of Western superiority, intellectual, technological, industrial, to other parts of the world is truly exposed when we discover that Western achievements are founded upon, and have grown out of, the inventions and scientific/technological discoveries of Asian and African cultures. For example, astronomy, mathematics, the concept of zero, geometry, geography, cartography, zoology, botany, medicine, the alphabet, philosophy, humanism, metaphysics, agriculture, etc., as well as ingenious inventions such as the wheel, bricks, glass, iron, the triangular lateen sail, bronze casting, etc., were all first invented or discovered in Egypt, Arabia, Mesopotamia, Chaldea, India, Persia, or China. Many of our domesticated animals (including the cow, horse, pig, dog, cat, and sheep), most of our flowers, fruits and vegetables, the rabbit, most of our poultry, and many perfumes, were brought over from Asia or Africa to Europe by the Ancient Greeks, the Romans and the Crusaders. Algebra is an Arabic word ('Al-Kebra') as is the word chemistry and the names of stars, such as Algol, Aldebaran and Bootes.

Much of the West's philosophy and religious beliefs were transmitted there from the East, such as the concept of monotheism (Jewish monotheism influenced Greek thinking and the concept of God in classical Greek philosophy), Christianity (which is based on the holy books of the Jews, the Law of Moses, and the teachings of Jesus and Paul, all Jews), the Bible, the ideas of Zoroaster, etc. Most of the world's ethical prophets came from the East, including Moses, Jesus, Buddha, Mohammed, and Confucius.

Many of the West's inventions and technological discoveries were pre-empted by the Ancient Chinese, such as the harness, the sternpost rudder, the magnetic compass, the blast-furnace (later developed into steam power by the West to drive the Industrial Revolution), paper, paper maps, printing, silk, irrigation, the crossbow, gunpowder, the horizontal loom, the spinning-wheel, cast-iron, etc. Indeed, in the words of the author Willem Hendrik Van Loon, '...that much-vaunted progress of the West is merely a continuation of the progress that was begun in the East. It is highly doubtful whether the West would have been able to go ahead if it had not learned the rudiments of everything it knows in the schools of the East.

'The knowledge of the Greeks was not the result of cerebral spontaneous combustion. Mathematics and astronomy and architecture and medicine did not, like Pallas Athene, jump forth from the head of Zeus, armed from head to foot, ready for the glorious battle upon human stupidity. They were the result of slow and painful and deliberate growth, and the real pioneering work was done along the banks of the Euphrates and the Tigris... [as well as the Ganges and the Indus and the Yellow River and the Nile] (Hendrik Van Loon *History of Man*).

The West and the East need to acknowledge their long cultural and historical relationship, often creative and affirmative. A scholar, a member of the 'Brethren of Purity', who lived in tenth-century Basra, in present-day Iraq, said in hope, 'If one could combine Arabic faith and Jewish intelligence with an Iraqi education, Christian conduct, Greek knowledge, Indian mysticism and a Sufi way of life, this would be the perfection of humanity.' (Wood, *Legacy: A Search for the Origins of Civilisation*)

Atheism, Darwinism and scientific materialism in practice have proved to be as intellectually conformist, narrow-minded, bigoted, oppressive, repressive and destructive as organised religion. Lenin was a staunch atheist, rationalist, logical positivist, secularist and materialist who did not believe in metaphysics, spirituality, any 'higher reality' or experience of a 'beyond'. Atheism and materialism were the only creeds allowed in Bolshevik Russia and anyone who did not conform was expelled, persecuted or forced into silence. In 1922 over 200 'undesirable' intellectuals and religious philosophers were expelled from the Soviet Union. Only conformity to atheist and materialist dogma was permitted in Bolshevik Russia. By expelling religion and metaphysics from the Soviet Union Lenin believed he was thereby freeing Russia from superstition, prejudice, sentimental idealism, conservatism and inefficiency, but this unwittingly led to the destruction of moral individualism, transcendental values, faith and individual 'inner' freedom, and ultimately a totalitarian state.

Adolf Hitler was a staunch Darwinist who believed in the survival of the fittest. His philosophy of evolution propounded the idea of evolutionary fitness. The stronger, healthier and more intelligent races had the right to rule over, enslave or exterminate those who were less fit. The superior race of Aryans was to become a race of iron-willed supermen, and any moral individualism, transcendental values, conscience, compassion or individual 'inner' freedom were seen as sentimental weaknesses. Thus cruelty, barbarity, ruthlessness, ethnic cleansing and genocide were acceptable and morally right if these means justified the ends, that is, the creation of a race of supermen, who were the fittest in an evolutionary sense to rule the world. Darwin's amoral philosophy of survival of the fittest justified the Nazis' perverted beliefs and ruthlessness. This also occurred in the Soviet Union under Stalin, who also believed the ends justified the means, and sacrificed untold millions on the altar of the Soviet Utopia where science and technology would create a heaven on earth for humankind. It has been said that the 'battle for metallurgy' and rapid industrialisation in Stalin's Russia cost as many lives as the Battle of Stalingrad.

The worship of science, materialism and technology and the elimination of individual 'inner' freedom and transcendental or spiritual values was one of the gravest errors of the Soviet experiment. The worship of science and the cult of technology in order to form a secular Utopia or heaven here on earth (rather than in an afterlife, the Second Coming of Christ or Messianic Age) became the goal of Soviet life. Nature was seen as a kind of enemy to be conquered, manipulated and controlled. This Bolshevik philosophy was partly drawn from the ideas of the nineteenth century Russian philosopher Nikolai Fyodorov. Fyodorov viewed nature as an opponent which condemns human personality to extinction. Bolshevism also viewed humankind as destined for dominion over nature through technology and science. By applying technology and science to nature, society and people ('engineering of the human soul') humankind could create Utopia on earth, colonise space, and perhaps even achieve immortality. Fyodorov believed that humankind is the pinnacle of evolution and its potential creator and director. By directing evolutionary processes and regulating nature through scientific means humankind could achieve radical life extension, even physical immortality, as well as the resurrection of the dead, space and ocean colonisation, and the perfection of the human race and human society. He thought these should be the highest goals of science. Perhaps humankind could even emancipate itself from the earth itself through the conquest of space, where humanity could evolve into a superman and conquer the universe. But this Marxist-Fyodorovian cult of technology and science did not conquer either space or the earth, or defeat mortality. It achieved great strides forward (such as putting the first man in space) and some great engineering achievements but the cost to nature and the environment has been catastrophic, such as desertification, terrible pollution, and nuclear contamination from the

Chernobyl disaster. The application of science and technology in the Soviet Union failed to transmute the base metal of society, nature and human nature into gold.

Science is only truly intelligent when it recognises both spirit and matter. True intelligence reaches between the multiplicity of nature and the oneness of God connecting and uniting them. Einstein wrote, 'The most important function of science is to awaken the cosmic religious feeling and keep it alive'. He also wrote, 'I want to know God's thoughts…The rest are details.' God's thoughts can be touched by both science and by direct mystical or contemplative experience. But the fixed rigid dogmas of materialist science take away from the direct personal experience of the supreme oneness underlying all existence. Plato believed that the highest form of human activity was contemplation and to see the world rightly. Science is too bound up with business, politics, human frailty, greed and ego to see the world rightly. It is ignorant of the essential divinity of life. The Jewish magician Simon Magus taught that within each human soul there dwells an infinite power, which is the root of the universe.

Science is a useful tool but not a guiding principle of humankind's creative evolution. It has been said that we may as well worship a screwdriver if we rely on science for our universal truths. The interference and dogma of organised religion or cynical scientific materialism deprive human beings of their unique personal creative evolution. Organised religion and materialist science try to inscribe their own vision of truth and knowledge on the blank canvas of the human heart and mind. But perhaps the human heart and mind are not blank canvases, but we are born into this world 'Not in entire forgetfulness, And not in utter nakedness, But trailing clouds of glory' (Wordsworth) and our own truth is hidden within. It is our God-given right to seek our own truths and philosophy of life within and without the interference or dogma of either materialist science or organised religion. Each must perfect himself or herself in his or her own way, and free themselves of the nets of materialist science and organised religion which are flung out to catch us from flight. Artists, poets and philosophers try to fly by those nets to seek the truth beyond the surface and the shadow of the reality we call life. As Samuel Taylor Coleridge pondered,

'And what if all of animated nature
Be but organic Harps diversely fram'd,

That tremble into thought, as o'er them sweeps
Plastic and vast, one intellectual breeze,
At once the Soul of each, and God of all?
... These shapings of the unregenerate mind;
Bubbles that glitter as they rise and break
On vain philosophy's aye-babbling spring.'
(The Aeolian Harp, 1795)

Science and technology have proved to be good and useful intellectual and physical tools which have brought immense benefits and advancements in knowledge and understanding. They have helped to supply humankind's physical needs and wants. However, they have also brought in their wake terrible harm and havoc to the environment and to nature. In addition, they have disturbed humankind's spiritual, moral, and holistic values or insights, through the cults of materialism, scientism, reductionism, compartmentalisation, specialisation, and isolationism of disciplines. Science (which derives from the Latin word 'scientia' meaning 'knowledge') is only truly knowledgeable when it recognises it is only part of the whole of Creation. Materialist science standing alone as a complete and universal philosophy of life can only lead to humankind's moral, spiritual, imaginative, contemplative, poetic and philosophical pauperisation. Humankind possesses 'higher', spiritual and poetic intelligences, faculties or modes of perception, as well as intellectual or scientific ones, and both require expression and exploration for the full evolutionary expansion of the individual and humankind as a whole.

Or perhaps in this universe of ours there is no God, no deities, no metaphysics, no soul or spirit in anything, and no inner conscience (which Hitler cynically called a 'Jewish invention'). Perhaps all beliefs in spirituality or religion are inane, chimerical, superstitious fantasies, delusions and comforting myths. Perhaps the universe is a mechanism which runs without any external aid and there is nothing 'beyond' or a 'higher' reality. But that is of no concern or consequence to the poet, artist or philosopher since perhaps the material world itself is the delusion which hides the real world, other planes of existence, dimensions, levels of consciousness, 'nameless vortices of never-dreamed-of strangeness' and 'wild weird climes that lie sublime out of space and out of time' from our eyes. Is materialist science a delusion or is the experience of 'higher', religious or philosophical realities a delusion? Who knows? But we pauperise humankind and become intransigent fundamentalists when we proclaim there is only one truth about reality, naturally our own, or only one true faith, also our own, whether derived from materialist science or from organised religion. Science and religion cannot reveal all of life's mysteries, or explain the meaning of everything, and nor will they ever be able to do so, since they are insufficient in themselves. Science can go some way in explaining the material world and religion some way in discovering the spiritual world, but it takes philosophy, art and poetry to bridge the two and thus

'With sober Reason Faith unites
To vindicate the ideal rights
Of Human-Kind – the true agreeing
Of objects with internal seeing
Of effort with the end of Being.'
(William Wordsworth)